Hard Questions

edited by Frank Colquhoun

"Now when the queen of Sheba
heard of the fame of Solomon
she came to Jerusalem
to test him with hard questions..."

InterVarsity Press
Downers Grove, Illinois 60515

First American printing, March 1977

*© 1976 by CPAS and reprinted by
InterVarsity Press with
permission from the Church Pastoral
Aid Society, Falcon Court,
32 Fleet Street, London EC4Y 1DB.*

*InterVarsity Press is the book
publishing division of Inter-Varsity
Christian Fellowship, a student movement
active on campus at hundreds of
universities, colleges and
schools of nursing.
For information about local and regional
activities, write IVCF, 233 Langdon St.,
Madison, WI 53703.*

*ISBN 0-87784-720-7
Library of Congress Catalog
Card Number: 00-0000*

Printed in the United States of America

Contributors

Professor Sir Norman Anderson *O.B.E., Q.C., Ll.D., D.D., F.B.A.*

Canon T. F. C. Bewes *M.A.*

The Rev. Richard Bowdler *M.A.*

The Rev. Colin Brown *M.A., Ph.D.*

The Rev. Colin O. Buchanan *M.A.*

The Rev. Maurice C. Burrell *M.A.*

The Rev. Julian W. Charley *M.A.*

Canon Frank Colquhoun *M.A.*

Canon D. K. Dean *M.A., B.D.*

Canon O. K. de Berry *M.A.*

Canon G. H. Donne Davis *M.A.*

The Ven. T. Dudley-Smith *M.A.*

The Rev. John E. Goldingay *B.A.*

Canon E. M. B. Green

Douglas Jackson *M.A., M.D., F.R.C.S.*

The Rev. John C. King *M.A.*

Prebendary Geoffrey Lester *M.A.*

The Rev. R. C. Lucas *M.A.*

Professor D. M. Mackay *B.Sc., Ph.D., F.Inst.P.*

The Ven. G. J. C. Marchant *M.A., B.D.*

The Rev. R. E. Nixon *M.A.*

Canon J. F. C. O'Byrne *M.A., B.D.*

The Rev. J. I. Packer *M.A., D.Phil.*

The Rev. Martin Parsons *M.A.*

The Rev. Michael J. Saward *B.A.*

The Rev. John A. Simpson *M.A.*

Professor D. C. Spanner *Ph.D., D.Sc.*

The Rev. J. K. Spence *M.A.*

Canon J. Stafford Wright *M.A.*

The Rev. L. E. H. Stephens-Hodge *M.A.*

The Rev. J. R. W. Stott *M.A., D.D.*

The Ven. John B. Taylor *M.A.*

The Rev. A. C. Thiselton *B.D., M.Th.*

Professor A. P. Waterson *M.D., F.R.C.P.*

David Winter *B.A.*

The Rev. M. A. P. Wood *D.S.C., M.A.*

The Rev. T. E. Yates *M.A.*

Contents

Editor's Preface

The purpose of this collection is to make available in a compact, convenient form some plain biblical answers to the sort of questions which are commonly voiced by people today, both in the church and on the fringe.

Most of the questions dealt with are big ones and raise all sorts of issues. It is clear that within the limits laid down (roughly 1,000 words for each answer) the writers are not able to deal with the questions completely or adequately. Nor do they make any pretense of doing so. All they attempt here is to face the questions honestly and sympathetically in the light of modern trends of thought, to indicate the general lines of approach from a Christian viewpoint and to stimulate further thought and inquiry on the part of the reader.

The present volume is the first American edition of the newly revised edition (1976) of a book first published in 1967. I hope that what is offered now to American readers may provide some useful guidance to those who are faced with genuine difficulties in accepting or understanding the Christian faith, especially young people who are seeking a firmer foundation on which to build their Christian life.

As editor I must express my gratitude to all who have contributed to this book by providing material new and old. In particular I wish to thank the Venerable Timothy Dudley-Smith, now Archdeacon of Norwich, who was closely involved in the planning of the original edition, for the invaluable help he has given me in the task of revision. Finally, I gladly acknowledge the collaboration of the Rev. Robert Backhouse, Publications Secretary of the Church Pastoral Aid Society, and of his staff, in preparing the manuscript for the press and producing the book in its new format.

Norwich Cathedral
Canon Frank Colquhoun

1
How can we know God?

Less than a hundred years ago, Benjamin Jowett, Master of Balliol, is said to have thundered at a free-thinking undergraduate: 'Find a God by the end of the week or go down.' Most of us today are not faced with quite the same urgency but we are perplexed by much the same questions. Is there a God who may be known? we ask; and, Are there means by which we may begin to discover him?

To the first question the Bible attempts no answer at all. It starts with its great premise, that 'In the beginning God...'; and the Church of England begins the first of her Thirty-Nine Articles from the same standpoint: 'There is but one living and true God...' When A. E. Housman said of the Church of England that it was 'the best religion ever invented' because it eliminated 'so much Christian nonsense' he was unjust as much with the word *invented* as with the rest of his *bon mot*. True Christianity is not invented; it is revealed.

The short answer, in fact, to *How can we know God?* is *by what he chooses to reveal.* Paul works this out in the first chapter of Romans, talking of the pagans of his day.

For what can be known about God is plain to them because God has shown it to them. Ever since the creation of the world his invisible nature, namely, his eternal power and deity, has been clearly perceived in the things that have been made.
(Romans 1:19-20)

God known in his works
Of course you need to have eyes to see God in his works. Those who wish not to trace his hand in nature will almost certainly have their wish granted. The verdict of Sherlock Holmes, quoted below, is considered almost as the prototype of dispassionate but keen observers:

There is nothing in which exact deduction is so necessary as in religion. It can be built up as an exact science by the reasoner. Our highest assurance of the goodness of Providence seems to me to rest in the flowers. All other things – our powers, our desires, our food – are necessary for our existence. But the rose is an extra. Its smell and colour are an embellishment of life, not a condition of it. It is only goodness that gives extras.

One of God's works, of course, is yourself. In the very first of his *Broadcast Talks* (which is now reprinted as the first section of *Mere Christianity*) C. S. Lewis began with a vivid description of people quarrelling ('That's my seat, I was there first' – 'Leave him alone, he isn't doing you any harm'), and went on to demonstrate how even in quarrels we appeal to an innate Law or sense of fair play or standard, which is other than ourselves. More than this, most people at times are conscious of a 'spiritual sense' whose promptings are usually too faint to stir us, and never last for long, but sometimes – just sometimes – remind us that God has set eternity in man's heart.

God known in his messengers

We can only know as much of God as he is willing to show us of himself. The Old Testament is largely a record of how he set about revealing himself to his chosen people, the Jews, through the long course of history. Sometimes, particularly at the start, this is done in dramatic ways – in the burning bush, in the great deliverance at the Red Sea, in a pillar of fire or cloud. But soon we find that what God really wants to say (or show) to man is not to be learnt in earthquake, fire or tempest, which may picture a little of his power and greatness, but in the 'still small voice' that spoke to Elijah in a cave at Horeb, in which is the expression of justice and friendship, righteousness, concern and love.

The *prophets* is the term used to describe God's special messengers; and there are still 'prophets,' though of a rather different kind, at work to-day revealing God to man. Different, because these are 'the last days' described in the first verses of the letter to the Hebrews:

In many and various ways God spoke of old to our fathers by the prophets; but, in these last days he has spoken to us by a Son ... He reflects the glory of God and bears the very stamp of his nature ...   (Hebrews 1:1–3)

Jesus Christ is not a messenger bearing a faint reflection of God, as were the prophets. He is both the very Word of God to us, and also 'the brightness of his glory, and the express image of his person.'

God known in his Son

We know God to-day when we know Jesus Christ his Son. 'Have I been with you so long, and yet do you not know me, Philip?' asked

Jesus on the evening before he died, and went on to say: 'He who has seen me has seen the Father' (John 14:9 RSV). Our clearest picture of what God is like is Jesus Christ. And to know Christ, in a personal and vital way, is to know God. That same evening, in his great prayer to the Father, Jesus said, 'this is eternal life, that they know the only true God, and Jesus Christ whom thou hast sent' (John 17:3).

To 'know Christ' is not simply to know *about* him – to have 'O' levels (or even 'A' levels) in Religious Knowledge. As the Bible uses the word, it means a personal encounter, in which we place ourselves, sinners as we are, in the hands of Christ, and ask him to take our spoilt and selfish lives, and remake us as new men. The word the Bible uses for this experience – our 'coming to Christ' (*come* is a word found very often on his lips) and his promise – is '... him who comes to me I will not cast out' (RSV) or, in the New English Bible, '... the man who comes to me I will never turn away' (John 6:37).

God known in experience

God is only 'found' or 'known' when we enjoy with him a relationship of love – a relationship which Jesus frankly described in terms of Father and Son. We sometimes say, loosely, that 'God is like a Father,' but this is the wrong way round. The fact is that the best fathers are a little – it is only the most shadowy of hints – like God. *He* is the prototype. From him 'every family in heaven and on earth is named' (Ephesians 3:15).

God truly known will include not only the experience of his divine Fatherhood but the experience of Jesus Christ as Saviour from sin, Lord of life, and Companion on our way. It will include the experience of the indwelling Holy Spirit of God to inspire and strengthen us, and make us holy too. To find God in this way is better described as 'to become a Christian.' For this reason I commend to you the books and booklet listed at the end of this chapter, which set out, step by step, the means whereby, if you have never yet done so, you yourself can find and know God, and so become a Christian.

T. Dudley-Smith

Further reading:
What makes a man a Christian? by Timothy Dudley-Smith (Hodder)
Choose Freedom by E. M. B. Green (IVP)
The Living God by P. B. Coombs (Falcon)
Journey into Life by Norman Warren (Falcon)
My God is Real by David Watson (Falcon)

Isn't one religion
as good
as another?

'All Chinese look alike.' This complaint tells you at once two things about the speaker: first, that he is not himself Chinese (a safe bet!), and second, that he lacks interest in Chinese people generally, so that he never looks at any of them very hard. Similarly, if someone asks whether the world's religions are not for all practical purposes the same, it suggests first that he knows and cares little about religions in general, and second that he is not committed to any one religion in particular – for if he was, he would be sure that the answer to his question is *no*!

Commitment and judgment

But would a committed man be the right person to judge? Is not an uncommitted attitude a help to clearer discernment? No – not at the deepest level, anyway. So far from the uncommitted man being able to discern the truth about all religions, he cannot fully appreciate any of them. The onlooker is supposed to see most of the game, but in matters where commitment is involved mere detached observers make poor judges. It is those who have taken the plunge, not those who gather goose-pimples on the edge, who really know what the water is like. Bachelors cannot in the nature of the case be profound authorities on married life, nor the non-religious on religions.

The chances are that the question under discussion would only ever be asked by someone recoiling, in conscious non-acceptance, from the claims of one particular faith. Certainly, all the world's great religions do in fact claim to be true, final, and exclusive, and one of the marks of their adherents is that they make these claims their own, and show the courage of their convictions by judging that those who

14

reject these claims are, to that extent, wrong. No Jew, Christian, Moslem, or Buddhist could countenance the suggestion that one religion is as good as another. This must be stressed at the outset.

Good for what?

The more one thinks about the suggestion, the odder it seems. 'Good for what?' one asks. The great religions do not claim to be good for the same thing! Christianity points the road to endless fellowship with God; Buddhism and Hinduism profess only to plot the path to final personal extinction. Nor can it be blithely assumed, as is so often done, that we all worship the same God. Tribal religions are polytheistic, each with a different quota of deities; Hinduism is pantheistic; Buddhism is atheistic; and among monotheistic faiths, Judaism and Islam are as strongly unitarian as Christianity is Trinitarian!

A century ago, when comparative religion as a science was in its infancy, some German thinkers embraced the idea that there is a 'highest common factor' of religions, a sense of kinship with God which is common property, but which different religions express with varying degrees of adequacy. On this view, Christianity is certainly the Rolls-Royce among religions, the best of its kind, but the same sense of oneness with God underlies them all, just as the same basic design is found in all cars. Hence Kipling's sentiment: 'Many roads thou hast fashioned; all of them lead to the light.' Or, as one often hears it put: 'We're all climbing the same mountain; we shall meet at the top.' Hence, too, the sustained quest, in certain university exam papers, for 'the definition of religion,' as if the heart of religion everywhere was the same. However, closer study of non-Christian faiths in this century has shown that the likenesses between them and Christianity are on the surface only; in basic outlook they are poles apart from the faith which acknowledges Jesus of Nazareth as divine Saviour and Lord, and as such, God's last word to man.[1]

Some might answer the question 'Good for what?' by saying 'Good for meeting certain universally felt needs' – such as the need for inner tranquillity and detachment. This is to reduce all religion to do-it-yourself psychiatry, or yoga – psycho-physical self-culture. The claim made by all religions, however, is to bring a true message about the universe and the powers behind it, and to show the way of adjustment, not merely to yourself, but to your whole cosmic environment. And the fact we must face is that the messages are at variance, so that you have to choose between them. Not more than one of them can be true.

The uniqueness of Christianity
This is the place to stress the uniqueness of Christianity, which differs
more radically from other world-religions than any of them differ
from each other. Old preachers spoke of the 'three Rs' of the gospel:
Ruin, Redemption, and *Regeneration*. Under these headings the most
distinctive features of Christianity fall.

Ruin   Other faiths assume our ability to secure and retain God's
favour by right action, and give us detailed guidance as to how to do
it; but Christianity says that sin has so ruined us that we cannot do
this. It is beyond our power to keep the law of God as we should; we
are guilty and helpless, wholly unable to save ourselves, and so must
be saved, if at all, by the action of another (Romans 8:8, 9:30–10:13;
Galatians 2:21, 3:10–12; Ephesians 2:1–9; Titus 3:3–7).

Redemption   Other faiths direct us to follow the teaching of their
founders, famous men long deceased; but Christianity, identifying its
founder as God incarnate, who died for our sins and rose again to
bestow forgiveness, proclaims him as alive and calls on us to trust him
and his atoning work, making him the object of our worship and
service henceforth. Despite various pagan myths (which C. S. Lewis
called 'good dreams') about saviours of one kind or another,
redemption through the love of the son of God, who became man,
bore his father's judgment on our sins, and rose from death to reign
for ever, is a theme without parallel in the world's religions (Romans
3:23–26, 4:24 *f*., 5:6–10; Galatians 2:20, 3:13 *f*.; 2 Corinthians
5:18–21; 1 John 4:8–10; Revelation 5; Acts 16:30 *f*.).

Regeneration   Christianity proclaims that those who repent of sin and
trust in Jesus Christ are created anew at the heart of their being by the
Holy Spirit. They are united to Jesus Christ in his risen life; their
inner nature is changed, so that their deepest impulse is not now to
disobey God and serve self, but to deny self and obey God. Thus they
are born again into a new life of fellowship with Christ, assurance of
forgiveness and sonship to God, and unconquerable hope and joy.
There is nothing like this in any other religion (John 3:3–15; Romans
6:1–14, 8:16–39; Corinthians 5:14–17; Colossians 2:10–15, 3:1–4; 1
Peter 1:3–13).

The Christian picture of other religions
A final unique feature of Christianity is that, though other religions
do not explain it, it explains them. In Romans 1:18–25 Paul accounts
for the prevalence of idolatory in terms of sinful man the world over
suppressing and distorting the 'general revelation' of God and his

claims as Creator which is given to us in and with our knowledge of created things. Paul sees man as having an inescapable sense of God which obliges him to worship something, yet as having an antipathy to God, induced by sin, which impels him not to worship the God who made him. So he distorts and falsifies the knowledge of God given him in general revelation. Hence spring the many forms of non-Christian religion, all containing details that are right in an overall setting that is wrong, and all conspicuously lacking knowledge of God's forgiveness in Christ, of which general revelation tells nothing.

Scripture does not regard non-Christian religion as saving. Jesus Christ must be proclaimed to all the world, and men everywhere must be called to turn 'to God from idols, to serve a living and true God' through Jesus' mediation (1 Thessalonians 1:9 RSV), for 'there is no other name under heaven given among men by which we must be saved' (Acts 4:12).

J. I. Packer

1 For evidence which shows this, see *The World's Religions*, (IVP) edited by J. N. D. Anderson.

3

Can we still take the Bible seriously today?

Why do miners attach such importance to their lamps? Why does the captain of a fogbound ship attach such importance to his radar? Or why have Christians ever attached such importance to the Bible? Clearly, by these means certain vital information is directly and reliably available, and without them there would only be darkness and confusion.

In a dense fog some may guess their way – and the world is full of 'guessed' religions. Most Englishmen make up their own religion and it tells them first that the ideal code of conduct is the one they already have, second that their religion is their own, neither to be corrected by others nor imposed on others, and thirdly that everything will be all right in the long run. That is like the easy guess of the car driver who runs into a fogbank and decides to keep going straight on. It is an easy guess, but is it a right one?

Divine revelation

As Christians we do not guess. God has spoken – and spoken clearly – in the events of history, through the voice of his prophets, and by the coming into this world of his Son Jesus Christ. This is how the writer of the Epistle to the Hebrews puts it:

When in the former times God spoke to our forefathers, he spoke in fragmentary and varied fashion through the prophets. But in this the final age he has spoken to us in the Son whom he has made heir to the whole universe, and through whom he created all orders of existence. (Hebrews 1:1–2 NEB)

All Christian faith rests on the basis of divine revelation and the Bible is the authoritative record of that revelation. Hence Christians accept the Bible as the written Word of God which bears witness to Christ

18

the incarnate Word of God. This is the supreme value of the Bible and its unique importance for the Church.

If this statement of the Christian case is true, it is no less true because we live in the twentieth century. God does not change his nature from one year to the next. Sciences change in their context, scope, methods, and results, but theology (the study of the nature of God and his relations to men) does not. Theological books of a century ago are often still very useful – few textbooks in the sciences are. But a problem *has* arisen. The Christian Church has itself become uncertain about the Bible. This uncertainty lies around us like a mist today. It is helpful to look at its origins and see whether it cannot be dispelled.

Interpretation

Perhaps the greatest problem is the question of interpretation. Christians who believe the Bible are often accused of 'taking the whole Bible literally.' We don't, of course. The proper way to 'take' the Bible is *naturally*. Each part has its own *natural* idiom – parable is parable, poetry is poetry, apocalyptic is apocalyptic, sober history is sober history. Obviously some facts are not literal. Shall we have harps in heaven, for instance? I doubt it – but I do not therefore disbelieve the Book of Revelation; I rather seek the key to unlock its admittedly difficult idiom. The early chapters of Genesis are similar – rather like a backward-looking Book of Revelation. Christians are probably no wiser to contend for a literal seven days in Genesis than they would be to contend for literal harps in Revelation.

Interpretation is obviously hardest where the Bible portrays situations at the furthest distance from our present experience – the ordinary language of everyday experience is stretched to breaking-point to convey it. So we can still believe in the Bible, whether or not we interpret such passages adequately. The difficulty has been that Christians have in the past tended to bind together a literal interpretation of the difficult passages with the truth of the Bible, so that they stood or fell together. They duly fell. But they need not have done, if they had not been bound together. In that case the failure of one line of interpretation would merely have started the hunt for another and better one.

The Bible as history

A large part of the Bible is, however, literal history (though history seen as God's actions and the outworking of his purpose). And this has led to uncertainty where men have denied its credibility as *history*. It has been conventional to decry the stories in the books of Moses, on the ground that they were not written down till several centuries after the events they record. But this is only a theory about the literary construction of the books. It would not, if true, automatically rule out the historical truth of the stories. And it is in fact unproven. It has many difficulties even as a theory. Many scholars today are less certain than they used to be about its plausibility. The theory often originated or took its growth from a supposition (indeed, a pre-supposition) that the knowledge of God could not have been so highly developed in the time of Moses as the books of Moses say it was. But this presupposes that the knowledge of God had to evolve slowly, and excludes the dramatic intervention of God which books claim happens. Theories like this are often accepted as the 'assured results of modern scholarship,' even at a time when modern scholarship is itself discarding or at least rewriting the theories so acclaimed.

The question of whether or not God could or did dramatically intervene in the affairs of men is raised in an even more critical way when the history of Jesus Christ himself, as recorded in the Bible, is investigated. Can scientific evidence be brought to bear in the story of the Virgin Birth or of the Resurrection? Some men talk as though science had 'disproved' these events. But the only possible 'disproof' would be the conclusion of an inquiry which started with a presupposition like, for example, 'Dead men don't rise.' They don't of course (or, at least, not yet!). But does this decide the issue when the Bible says that the Son of God rose from the dead? If Jesus was the Son of God, what happens when the Son of God dies? There is no scientific evidence that can throw light on this. It is a totally unique event. Its truth cannot be decided by 'probabilities.' Belief or disbelief alike arise from a man's presuppositions. Some approach the Bible with minds open to learn what it says, others with minds shut by scepticism and thus not prepared to believe in unique events.

Morality
A further problem is the question of morality. Do we *like* the God revealed in the Bible? Does he conform to our notions of morality? For example, is judgment a sufficiently attractive theme for us to believe in a God who practises it? This is the hardest question of all – far harder than questions about details of history. There is an emotional longing for a God who is all kindness, and this longing when projected into the biblical record gives rise to uncertainties about the Bible, because clearly the God of the Bible is not *just* kindness and goodwill.

However, the truth of the world around us compels us to think again. The true God has a certain sternness of character, if he is true at all. He *is* love, but he is not only love. The starkest warnings of God's judgment come from Jesus himself and are warp and woof with the whole biblical message about him – we cannot dismember that unity for the sake of throwing out parts of his character we do not like.

An urgent need

A brief overall look at these and other uncertainties will suggest that the Bible is not rejected or doubted first on the offered ground that God would not reveal himself this way. The objection is rather that the *contents* of the Bible are unacceptable, for whatever reasons. It is biblical Christianity which is being doubted.

But without the Bible there is no Christianity, or only the dying remnants of it. God is the same today, or two thousand years ago, or a hundred years ago; men are the same also, and God still reveals himself to men by the Bible today. To take the Bible seriously is an even more urgent task for Christians in England just because the Christian foundations of our society are crumbling and collapsing. New humanist or secular presuppositions replace them. As society at large reflects the truth of God less and less, so the Christian must recover from the Bible a first-hand awareness of what God in Christ is like. In the face of an unbelieving world we do not abandon the Bible and try to remodel the nature of God – as if we could! Only by closer adherence to the Bible can we be truly enlightened by the knowledge of God, and so also be truly useful to society.

Colin Buchanan

4

Is there any value in reading the Old Testament?

The question is almost certainly born of frustration at one's first attempt to understand the Old Testament. Ancient history, repetitive language, bloody battles, dull and seemingly irrelevant prophesyings, all wrapped up in King James's English – and the bravest heart is inclined to melt. Far easier to swim in the clearer waters of the New Testament which is, after all, about Jesus Christ, the centre of our faith.

But on closer reading it is not *so* easy to understand the New Testament by itself. It abounds in technical terms, for instance, all of which need to be explained by reference to the teaching of the Old Testament. And even in the Gospels (which are relatively free of technicalities) a knowledge of Old Testament background is essential to understanding the teaching Jesus was trying to get across. So then the first part of an answer to our question is quite simple:

The Old Testament is the dictionary for the Jew
The list of New Testament words which need the Old Testament to explain them is immense; for example: *sacrifice, atonement, propitiation, redemption, righteousness, holiness, faith, covenant, passover, leaven,* and so on, to say nothing of all the many titles which were given to our Lord. Almost every important idea expressed in the New Testament has a long history of meaning behind it, and that meaning is to be found in the Hebrew Scriptures and nowhere else.

Let me give an illustration. Christ is described more than once in the New Testament as the 'lamb of God.' What does that mean to today's reader? To me it conjures up the picture of a lovable, innocent creature gambolling in a field ('all of an April evening' and

22

all that) or lying cuddled in someone's arms like a domestic pet. Not a very complete picture of the Saviour of the world, you may say. But that is the inevitable image suggested, *if you ignore the Old Testament.*

A look at the Old Testament, however, will show you something very different – a lamb before an altar: innocent, yes; silent and uncomplaining, certainly, but about to be sacrificed to atone for the sins of the man who is standing beside it with his hand resting on the poor victim's head. *Now* you can see the sinless Son of God, laying down his life without complaint or resentment, so that all who identify themselves with him and stand alongside him in faith may have their sins forgiven. The Lamb of God indeed!

But of course the Old Testament is much more than a glossary, or book of illustrations for New Testament terms, important though that function is. The very title *Christ = Messiah = Anointed One* reminds us that when God sent his Son into the world, he didn't simply thrust him into a religious vacuum; he sent him to a people who had been prepared for the event by at least two thousand years of history, a long succession of godly men and a fair-sized collection of writings which faithfully reflected God's nature and intentions.

The Old Testament is the introduction to the New

The public relations man knows that in these days you cannot just manufacture a new product and present it to the world, hoping it will be a success. Months of market-research, advertising, and sales-preparation are needed first. That may not be a very suitable illustration for a religious event, but God knew equally well that men's hearts needed to be conditioned for the coming of his Son. The Old Testament was this preparation for the Jewish people, and because of it Jesus could begin his ministry confident of two great facts: first, that his hearers had a true awareness of God and what he was like and what he required (though of course they had much still to learn); and second, that they had a deeply ingrained sense of right and wrong based on their religious background from the days of Moses and the Ten Commandments.

The Old Testament can do the same for every generation. Its teaching about sin and righteousness, about God's justice and holiness, about sacrifice and forgiveness – all these things help to condition men's hearts for the message of the gospel.

The Old Testament was Jesus' Bible

That, of course, is no argument to those who care nothing for Jesus, though it is quite an interesting fact that a man of his quality should have been moulded by what to the unbeliever is such an unpromising book. To the Christian, however, our Lord's devout use of the Old Testament and his regard for its teaching send him straightaway back to its pages to find out for himself how this strange collection of books made such an impact on the Son of God. He will find that Jesus soaked himself in it, memorizing large sections so that he could quote it at will. He used it as his final authority – as the Father's own Word, in fact – in arguments with his enemies and in conflict with the devil. He moulded his own life on its teaching and was especially guided by it in working out his messiahship and his eventual death, for which Isaiah 53 was his pattern (*cf* Luke 22:37). For Jesus, what the Bible said, God said.

And just to kill the lie that he thought like that because all Jews of his time did, and he was therefore nothing more than a child of his age, remember that when he had risen from the dead and was released from the limitations of his humanity, he spent much of his all too brief ministry to his friends in showing them 'in all the scriptures' – *ie* the Old Testament – 'the things concerning himself' (Luke 24:27). It really was as important as that.

So the Christian reads the Old Testament to learn more about the New Testament and to learn more about Christ. True, it is not easy. He may need the help of a commentary or Bible-reading notes; he will probably want to use another translation like the Revised Standard Version or the New English Bible to help him understand the sense. His greatest asset, however, will be the fact that he has a personal knowledge of Jesus Christ, who is himself the key to the Old Testament, and he has the Holy Spirit as his guide to make it live.

John B. Taylor

5

Are the Gospels historically reliable?

Christianity is unashamedly an historical religion. That is why the reliability of the Gospels is an important matter.

The authenticity of the documents
Our first question must be, 'Have we got the Gospels substantially as they were written, or have people tampered with them down the centuries?' Well, we are in a better position to assess the authenticity of the New Testament than of any other ancient document. The gap between the writing of Thucydides' *History* and the oldest manuscript we have of it is some 1500 years; in the case of Tacitus it is 800.

In striking contrast, we have manuscripts of all the Gospels written before AD 200, that is to say within a century of the originals. Indeed, we have a fragment of John's Gospel that experts date as early as AD 125. Thus the famous archaeologist, Professor Kenyon, could write,

... the interval between the dates of the original composition and the earliest extant evidence becomes so small as to be negligible, and the last foundation for any doubt that the Scriptures have come down to us substantially as they were written has now been removed.[1]

Non-Christian evidence
'Very well,' you may say, 'but what non-Christian evidence is there to back up what the Gospels say?' There are three answers to that: the evidence of the pagans, the Jews and of archaeology.

Pagan writers
You would not expect there to be much evidence in pagan writers about an obscure carpenter who lived in a backward province of the

empire. But there is some.[2] The Roman historian Tacitus, writing about AD 100, records Nero's persecution of Christians. 'The name of Christian,' he says, 'comes to them from Christ, who was executed in the reign of Tiberius by the procurator, Pontius Pilate' (*Annals*, 15:44). Suetonius, writing about AD 120, knows that Jews were expelled from Rome as early as AD 49 through quarrelling over one Chrestus[3] (*ie* Christus – they were pronounced the same).

The fullest account of Christian activities seen through Roman eyes comes to us in a long letter from Pliny the Younger, Governor of Bithynia about AD 110. He tells us of the spread of Christianity even in that far away province to such an extent that the pagan temples had to close down. He tells us that these Christians were not guilty of any wickedness, but used to gather every morning to sing a hymn to Christ as God, and that they refused to bow down to the Emperor's statue or to deny the name of Jesus (*Epistles*, 10:96).

Jewish writings

The references in the Jewish writings are, of course, hostile to Jesus. They tell us that Jesus practised magic, deceived the people, healed the sick, had disciples, added to the Law, and was executed.[4] Thus the Jerusalem Talmud says: 'On the Eve of Passover they hanged Yeshu of Nazareth.' The Jewish historian Josephus, writing at the end of the first century, knows that Jesus was the brother of James, claimed to be the Messiah, worked miracles, was crucified under Pilate, and was reputed to have risen from the dead (see particularly *Antiquities*, 18:3:3.).

It is interesting that all these Jewish sources admit that Jesus performed miracles; but they attributed them to demonic powers, and sorceries learned in Egypt. (Is this indirect confirmation of Matthew 2:13 *ff*?)

Archaeology

Archaeology can help a little, too. It has thrown light upon the census recorded in Luke 2.[5] It has produced a fascinating Imperial edict, dated between AD 20 and 50, saying nobody must disturb the tombs of the dead. This was found in Nazareth, and looks very much like official reaction to the resurrection. Evidence of a Christian church (including the Lord's Prayer) was found in the Italian towns of Herculaeneum and Pompeii, overcome by the eruption of Mount Vesuvius in AD 79.

Recently Professor Sukenik,[6] a Jewish archaeologist discovered this scribbled prayer on a Jerusalem ossuary (bone-casket): 'Jesus, Jesus, let him arise.' The date? *Before* AD 50! Think of the implication of those simple words – the deity of Christ, the truth of the resurrection, and so on. Thus the broad historical reliability of the main events recorded in the Gospels can be substantiated from non-Christian sources.

Internal evidence

But what of the Gospels themselves?

The great thing to remember is that they are an entirely new literary *genre*. Obviously they are not biographies of Jesus. What biography would fail to tell us any of the physical features of its hero, pass over thirty years of his life without mention, or concentrate half the book on his death? They are not histories, either; thus the evangelists are not much interested in the chronology of the events they record. They are the proclamation of good news about Jesus whom his disciples had come to believe was God's Saviour, sent for all men.

How far can we rely on them?

Professor C. H. Dodd has shown, in his *Apostolic Preaching and its Development*, that much the same pattern of preaching can be found in all the different and independent strands which go to make up the New Testament. There can be little doubt that it faithfully represents the original Christian preaching about Jesus. Some of what the evangelists record can be checked. Thus the existence of eye-witnesses in the sixties, when Mark's Gospel appeared, is some guarantee of the truthfulness of his record – otherwise it would have been discredited. Now Mark's Gospel, as any commentary will tell you, is not only one of the main sources of Matthew and Luke; it records the preaching of Peter. Thus it takes us back to the very earliest Christian message.

Again, had the Church 'cooked up' the contents of the Gospels, we would have expected to find them putting into Jesus' mouth matters of burning interest to themselves. But on the contrary, we find that the concerns of the early Church (the Lordship of Jesus, the Holy Spirit, the Jew-Gentile split, the circumcision issue, and so on) are conspicuous by their absence. Again, why make Jesus speak in parables, if he did not? Nobody in the early Church used parables, but the evangelists knew well that Jesus did. Nobody in the early Church called Jesus 'Son of Man,' but they knew he had used this title of himself. Indeed, although the evangelists felt free to alter the setting of Jesus' sayings, they paid meticulous respect to the sayings themselves. This suggests that the words of Jesus were, from the earliest times, treated as sacrosanct by the Church.

But how about John? Surely that is late and unreliable?

In recent years that estimate has had to be radically altered. For one thing, the sort of language used by Jesus in John ('children of light', 'doing the truth', etc.), so far from being, as was once thought, a mark of lateness, has now been discovered in the Dead Sea Scrolls, a hundred years or so before John's Gospel was written.

Furthermore, recent excavations have shown that John's Gospel is incredibly accurate, even where it seemed to be the reverse. Thus critics used to laugh at the Pool of Bethesda – there was no trace of it on the ground or in ancient literature. But now the pool has been discovered, and the name too has turned up in one of the Dead Sea Scrolls! Again, John's statement that Jesus was tried at a place called Gabbatha, the 'place of the pavement' (John 19:13), was disbelieved, and regarded as unhistorical embroidery. No one knew anything about such a pavement, until Père Vincent dug it up, some 20 feet below the surface of Jerusalem. It is 50 yards square, and was part of the Roman barracks of Antonia, destroyed in the fall of Jerusalem in AD 70 ... and not seen again till 1934. That means that this information of John's Gospel comes from before AD 70; not so late and unreliable after all! Indeed, St John's Gospel is now thought, by some leading modern scholars, to have been formed, even if not actually written, before AD 60.

There is no space to go further into this fascinating subject. If you want more, read Professor F. F. Bruce's book, *The New Testament Documents: Are they Reliable?* (IVP) or A. M. Hunter's *According to John* (SCM).

Michael Green

1 *The Bible and Archaeology*, page 288.
2 It is well set out in R. Dunkerley, *Beyond the Gospels* (Pelican, 1957).
3 *Life of Claudius*, 25.
4 See further the Jewish scholar Joseph Klausner, *Jesus of Nazareth* (1929).
5 *Was Christ born at Bethlehem?* by W. M. Ramsay (1898).
6 New Testament Studies (1956).

6

How could Jesus be both the child of Mary & the Son of God?

It was an astonishing conclusion reached by the first disciples, that Jesus was both Man and God. There were plenty of instances in pagan religions of a god appearing in human form, but that the god had *become* man – never! The very idea was without precedent. How, then, did this Christian conviction arise?

In his life

For those who left their fishing-boats at the call of Jesus to become his first followers there was never any doubt that he was human, though undoubtedly he was an unusual person. He experienced hunger and thirst, anger and grief, exhaustion and pain. But he also performed miracles, spoke with divine authority, and lived a perfect blameless life.

Their close association with him culminated in that memorable occasion at Caesarea Philippi when Peter cried out, 'You are the Christ, the Son of the living God' (Matthew 16:16). Experience had convinced them that here was no mere man but the very Son of God; and this conviction was confirmed unforgettably by the resurrection.

Only the Gospels of Matthew and Luke contain an account of the birth of Jesus. The details must have been supplied chiefly by Mary. The angel had said, 'the child to be born will be called holy, the Son of God' (Luke 1:35). It was not the sort of information that she would be likely to divulge till the resurrection had authenticated it, that Jesus had had no human father but been conceived by the Holy Spirit. It must have been Mary's evidence which strengthened still further the disciples' conviction about Jesus' divinity.

After Pentecost
When the disciples began to preach after Pentecost, they soon encountered opposition from Jew and Gentile alike. Their message was ridiculed (1 Corinthians 1:23). To present it rationally and convincingly, much thought was given to the theological significance of the events of Jesus' life. The fact required explanation. Thus the writer to the Hebrews asserts that God's Son, bearing 'the very stamp of his nature', assumed Man's nature also (Hebrews 1:2–3, 2:14). Only so could he do for man what man could not do for himself. The purpose of the Incarnation (God becoming Man) was atonement (God rescuing Man), which involved the shedding of his blood (Hebrews 9:22). Or again, Paul explains that there is 'one mediator between God and men, the man Jesus Christ' (1 Timothy 2:5). Because he was God and Man, he alone could represent both sides. Indeed, without the Incarnation the atonement itself would be unjust, if not impossible. So the personal conviction of the disciples, endorsed by the evidence of Mary, was seen to be both reasonable and necessary.

Such a conclusion pointed to the uniqueness of Jesus. If his supernatural birth and resurrection attested his divine origin, he was no less unique in his humanity. Neither friend nor foe could detect any moral fault in him, and he never betrayed any consciousness of sin within himself. 'Which of you convicts me of sin?' he asked (John 8:46), and there was no reply. It is essential to remember this, when we query how Jesus could have been both the child of Mary and the Son of God. To reason from our own experience of sinful humanity that he could not have been both is to forget that it is only in Jesus that we can see what true and perfect humanity is like. To deny the Christian claim is to ignore the evidence; to deny its possibility is to argue from false premises.

The early church
The early church discovered that various heresies arose when this truth was not adequately safeguarded, so they carefully defined it at the Council of Chalcedon in AD 451. But definition involved speculation, because the Incarnation was a unique event and the New Testament merely stated the fact without explaining its mode. They had to resort to current philosophical terms like *substance*, the meaning of which has altered subsequently. Their desire was to safeguard the distinction of Deity and Humanity, Creator and Creature, in the one Person, Jesus Christ. Thus he had been able to say at one moment, 'My father is greater than I' (John 14:28), at another, 'I and my Father are one' (John 10:30). It was not that he

was God and Man successively, but both simultaneously. As Man, he *grew* in wisdom and stature; he asked questions in the temple in order to be informed; he did not know the hour of his return in glory (Mark 13:32). As God, he claimed to be the perfect revelation of the Father – 'He who has seen me has seen the Father' (John 14:9). He forgave sins. He offered eternal life.

The description of the 'self-emptying' of Jesus in Philippians 2:5–11 gives us a clue to follow. When he became Man, Christ still remained 'in the form of God': that is to say, he retained the essential attributes of God. It was not these of which he divested himself. Else what would have happened to the universe, which is upheld by his authoritative word (Hebrews 1:3; Colossians 1:17), if he had discarded his omnipotence during his time on earth? What he chose to forgo as Man was equality with the Father. Throughout his earthly life he refrained from exercising his divine powers, unless prompted by the Father to use them. In the wilderness temptation he *could* have turned the stones to bread. In the garden of Gethsemane he *could* have summoned twelve legions of angels to his rescue. We should probably understand similarly his admission of lack of knowledge on certain occasions, when on others he displayed an awareness of facts of which no one had told him, as in the case of the Samaritan woman at the well. Thus the authority of his teaching would not in any way be diminished. Being God as well as Man, he could draw upon infinite resources of knowledge and power in a way that was impossible for other men. Yet he was not two people but one fully integrated personality. Our nearest analogy, though very inadequate, is that of our conscious and subconscious minds.

As with our fifth-century predecessors, we can only hazard an explanation. A further generation may express it differently. What remains unchanged is the *fact* of the Incarnation, for which the evidence and the theological necessity are certain.

Julian Charley

Does the Virgin Birth really matter?

To clear the ground and prevent confusion it is essential to state as simply as possible what is meant by the Virgin Birth of Jesus. It means that Jesus was conceived in the womb of his mother, Mary, who was a virgin, through the agency of the Holy Spirit and that no human father was involved. So that our Lord's entry into the world was miraculous, just as was his departure from it. It should be noted that really the term 'Virgin Birth' is inaccurate. What is in fact meant is virginal conception. There is nothing to suggest that the actual *birth* was not normal. Our starting place for information must be the New Testament, and in particular the Gospels.

According to Luke

St Luke prefaces his account by the statement that he 'has gone over the whole course of these events in detail' and that he gives 'authentic knowledge about the matters' (Luke 1:3–4 NEB). This evangelist takes particular interest in women, especially the little band of women who were associated with Jesus in his ministry, some of whom had been witnesses of his death and had seen him alive afterwards. In the Acts of the Apostles he continues to mention them as being associated with the apostles in the beginnings of the Church. Among them was Mary the mother of Jesus. Clearly it must have been from these women, possibly from Mary herself, that Luke gained his information about the birth of Jesus. He was acknowledged as an historian as well as a doctor and in consequence was well fitted to record accurately. As a doctor he knew about the processes of generation and childbirth. His knowledge of biological processes presents no difficulty to him in recording the Virgin Birth of Jesus. He tells of the visit to Mary of the angel Gabriel who said that Mary would bear a son while still a virgin:

Then the angel said to her, '... You shall conceive and bear a son ...' 'How can this be?' said Mary, 'I am still a virgin.' The angel answered, 'The Holy Spirit will come upon you, and the power of the Most High will overshadow you; and for that reason the holy child to be born will be called "Son of God"'.   (Luke 1:31–35 NEB)

Luke records here that Mary was a virgin; that she conceived Jesus by the power of the Holy Spirit and not by the normal method of human generation; and that this holy child was the Son of God. The origin of the holy seed was therefore divine and not human. Mary conceives, that is she receives the holy seed from God, she nourishes it and in due time gives birth to the holy child Jesus. At the beginning of Luke 2, the evangelist sets out the birth and its circumstances in an account which is familiar to most people and need not be quoted.

According to Matthew

We turn next to Matthew's Gospel. It is clear from internal evidence that Matthew writes quite independently of Luke whose narrative he had not seen. Whilst Luke writes from Mary's viewpoint, Matthew writes from the point of view of Joseph. It is natural that Joseph would wish to put on record the facts as he knew them in order to clear Mary's name. So as a just man, who had been told of the manner in which Mary, his betrothed, had become pregnant, he made known the facts, which are recorded in Matthew 1 and 2.

In this testimony, simply told, we read of his suspicions, of the explanation he received, of his efforts to protect both mother and child, and of the guidance given him by God. He makes it clear that Mary remained a virgin at least until Jesus was born: 'He took Mary home to be his wife, but had no intercourse with her until her son was born' (Matthew 1:25 NEB).

The other New Testament writers

The question arises as to why Mark, Paul, and Peter are silent about the Virgin Birth. Mark has nothing to say about Jesus before his baptism. This does not imply he was ignorant of the events preceding the baptism, nor that Peter, from whom he derived so many of his facts, knew nothing of the Virgin Birth. It is likely that in this, the earliest Gospel, the time was not ripe for the fact to be recorded, and in view of this Mark omits any mention of the birth and boyhood of Jesus. In his preaching the apostle Peter was silent on a subject which would have introduced sharp criticism and controversy. He concentrated rather on the cross and resurrection of Jesus.

Paul had many battles on his hands and in the early days of the Christian Faith he is reticent about the birth and early life of Jesus, both in his preaching in the Acts of the Apostles and in his epistles. In the Epistle to the Galatians he states that Jesus was the Messiah, the promised seed of Abraham, but he does not say he was born of a virgin, but 'born of a woman' (Galatians 4:4 RV). It is evident that he did not wish to involve himself in controversies with the slanderers and blasphemers of Jesus.

The early Church

Even such a brief look at the New Testament evidence as this should lead most honest investigators to come to the conclusion that the Virgin Birth is recorded there. It is clear that the accounts of Luke and Matthew were accepted as true by the early Church. Ignatius writing in AD 110 says: 'The virginity of Mary, and her child-bearing, and in like manner the death of the Lord are three mysteries of loud proclamation.' This is supported by Justin Martyr and Aristides. From the second century it is accepted and stated in credal form.

Conclusion

Having looked at the New Testament statements and the evidence of the teaching of the early Church we are in a position to answer our question. The fact that the preaching of the apostles Peter and Paul in Acts does not include the Virgin Birth yet resulted in thousands of converts to the Christian faith shows that it is not fundamental to the Christian gospel. It is not among the basic grounds of the faith, but rather it is a dependent belief. Paul makes the fact of the incarnation clear in his epistles, especially in the classic passage, Philippians 2:5–8, yet he says nothing about the precise manner of it. Many came to believe in Jesus through the preaching of the apostles without any knowledge of the Virgin Birth, and many would have had the knowledge of Jesus through the epistles without knowing of this doctrine.

Nevertheless, the plain and unambiguous statements in the Gospels cannot lightly be set aside. Those who believed through the preaching would come to know the facts of the Virgin Birth and accept them as part of the faith. It seems illogical to accept the miraculous resurrection of our Lord, but to boggle at his miraculous conception in the womb of the Virgin. If other doctrines about Jesus are accepted because of the testimony of the Gospels, then it follows that this also must be believed.

G. H. Donne Davis

8

What is the truth about man and the 'fall'?

What on earth is wrong with us? You and I can conquer almost any material problem, down to releasing atomic energy, travelling through space, and watching what is happening on the opposite side of the world. Yet a simple little thing like saying *Yes* when we are well aware that we should say *No*, and breaking some humiliating habit, is as hard for us as it was for the Greeks.

Everybody has to accept the inner mess. What we have to try to explain is how the whole human race has come to be like this. You can ignore this question, and simply face the situation as it is, but a serious thinker knows that origins must have something to contribute to present experience.

The basic problem

The Christian doctrine of the fall supplies some answer, but to begin by arguing about Adam and Eve is a waste of time. We must first see what we can do with the original question, namely: *What is wrong with us?*

Fundamentally we are not masters of ourselves. We are divided personalities. The situation has never been better summed up than it is by St Paul in Romans 7:15: 'I do not understand my own actions. For I do not do what I want, but I do the very thing I hate.' We can get into all sorts of tangles by trying to define exactly what we mean by the 'I' that is confronted by the actions of another 'I', but St Paul's words make very good practical sense.

Suppose we look at it like this. Everyone from childhood has an inner commander-in-chief, who assumes responsibility for directing how the bodily, mental and spiritual life should be lived. This commander is an ideal, which is continually being translated into moment-by-moment decisions.

Unfortunately we are not only identified with the commander, but we are also the whole army down to the individual private, and the army has to carry out the decisions. Privates, platoons, and companies often choose to act on their own. I, on the side of the commander, keep ordering, reorganizing, punishing, and often meet some success in quelling the rebellion, but never manage to be supreme commander-in-chief in act as well as in name.

Often the commander takes the line of least resistance, and decides to lower his ideals for the campaign. Then perhaps the malcontents will be satisfied. But they are not. Once the commander has yielded an inch, they have him on the run, and the whole force deteriorates.

This is a sensible analogy of what most of us feel about ourselves. But why does all this happen? Can we find the answer in infancy experience? If we take a maladjusted delinquent and examine his childhood, we commonly find that his upbringing was either too authoritarian or over-lacking in moral standards. Either extreme tends to produce delinquents. In theory we should be able to balance authority and freedom so precisely as to guarantee complete perfection. We can only say that no one is even in sight of doing this.

One may of course blame society, and society includes family groups. The commander needs right ideals, and society's ideals are warped and may be imbibed by the small child. But even when a child grows up with noble ideals, he still knows the problem of living up to them.

We have spent some time describing the obvious. You and I have a conscience, or moral sense, which sets ideals that we often fail to attain. In this we differ from the rest of the animal world, for, even if some of our moral feelings and reactions can be classified by psychologists as conditioned reflexes, there remains a whole area of quiet moral idealism which is peculiar to man.

The biblical picture

So now we can turn to our other question about the origins of our moral situation. There is one point on which we can find a majority agreement. There must have been some point in history or pre-history at which a human being, or human beings, came into existence with a sense of moral claims. Either this man was as helpless as we are, or at this point he was able to respond to each moral demand as he realized it. Anthropology does not supply any verifiable answer, but the Bible comes down on the side of the second.

But note how the Bible views it. The Bible is not satisfied with the definition of man as a tool-making animal. Certainly there were manlike creatures, using tools and fire, going back for perhaps half a million years or more. But Genesis introduces us to man in the likeness of God, with a spiritual capacity for knowing God, and the ability to obey or disobey.[1] The story of the fall in Genesis 3 is the story of how, when confronted with a specific issue, man and woman chose to be their own centre of good and evil. This amounted to being off-centre, and disorganized the inner being of man, for man can only be perfect if God is at the centre of his being.

So man said *No* to God, and fell into sin, which is both rebellion against God and also a state of inner rebellion against the commander who now tries to take the place of God. The Bible now becomes the story of man's restoration in Jesus Christ.

Theologians use the term *total depravity* to describe the present state of man. This does not mean that everyone is as bad as he could possibly be. Some 'commanders' produce more satisfying results in personal and society life than others do. But the term means that there is no single part of man's being that is wholly exempt from the effects of rebellion. The illustration is often used of poison in a cup of water. The quantity of poison need not be 100%, but not a single drop of the water can be drunk without swallowing poison. None of the drops of water that make up our physical, mental, or spiritual capacities are pure enough to become the river of life. This is what frustrates reformers who aim for the perfect society through the panacea of such things as politics, education, money, physical exercises, diet, or diving into the unconscious.

The Christian is certainly concerned with all human betterment, but he knows that renewal can come only through Christ becoming integrated into the control centre. Just as 'in Adam' (*ie* by birth) we are fragmented, so 'in Christ' we can be pulled together into God-centred unity. The process may begin suddenly with conversion, but it must be followed by steady Christ-centred growth.

If we all share the effects of the fall, are we responsible for our sins? Whatever the theory, in practice we do feel responsible for most of our wrong actions, and have feelings of guilt which can be removed only through forgiveness, and forgiveness comes through the sacrificial death of Jesus Christ. If we take the credit for our good deeds, we must accept the blame for the bad.

J. Stafford Wright

1 The historical background of Genesis 1–3 may be studied in *Who was Adam?* by E. K. Victor Pearce (Paternoster Press).

9

Was it necessary
for Jesus to die
on the cross?

Well, why did Jesus die? That is the real question. Some folk would have no difficulty in giving their answer. 'He died,' they would say, 'because he was a preacher of revolutionary doctrines. He disturbed the conventions of his contemporaries, aroused their jealousy, and exposed their hypocrisy, so they had him liquidated. He died as a martyr to his own greatness.'

Of course, there is truth in this theory, but it is by no means the whole truth. It ignores one great significant fact in the Gospel narratives, namely that Jesus went to the cross of his own deliberate purpose. No man took his life from him. He says 'I have power to lay it down, and I have power to take it again' (John 10:18). He refused to let Peter defend him in the garden, affirming that if he were to lift but a finger, the Father would immediately send more than twelve legions of angels to defend him. And when Pilate began to be a bit truculent, Jesus quietly said to him, 'You would have no power over me unless it had been given you from above' (John 19:11).

Why did he do it?
If then the death of Jesus was self-determined, what is its meaning? If he was not only given up to death by wicked men, but rather gave himself voluntarily to die, why did he do it?

Many explanations have been given. He died to reveal the inexhaustible love of God for sinners (eg Romans 5:8). He suffered to give us an example of patient fortitude under provocation (eg 1 Peter 2:18–23). He died to conquer evil by refusing to resist it by force. He also triumphed in the cross over all the cosmic powers of darkness (Colossians 2:15). All these statements are true, but none of them receives the greatest emphasis in the New Testament. The New Testament authors stress the connection between Christ's death and our sins. Had not he himself said, 'This is my blood of the new covenant, which is poured out for many for the forgiveness of sins' (Matthew 26:28)? So Paul echoed, 'Christ died for our sins in accordance with the scriptures' (1 Corinthians 15:3), and the apostle Peter added, 'Christ died for sins once for all, the righteous for the unrighteous, that he might bring us to God' (1 Peter 3:18). 'God … loved us,' wrote John, 'and sent his Son to be the expiation of our sins' (1 John 4:10).

The New Testament teaches then that it was for the forgiveness of our sins that Jesus Christ died, and that on the cross he achieved something objective and decisive by which the sins of the world may be forgiven.

Wasn't there another way?

But why, someone asks, could not God simply have pardoned our sins without all this fuss and bother? Why was Christ's death necessary? Anselm would have answered, 'You have not yet considered how serious sin is.' Or as another writer put it: 'Forgiveness, which to man is the plainest of duties, to God is the profoundest of problems.' If we sin against a human being it is a purely personal injury, and it is his duty to forgive us. But if we sin against God it is not just a personal offence involving two private parties: it is an infringement of the divine law. It throws the whole moral order out of gear.

What can God do? God is not omnipotent in the sense that he can do absolutely anything. God can only do those things which are consistent with his nature. He cannot therefore readily pardon the sinner, because he is a God of infinite justice. But neither can he readily punish the sinner, because he is also a God of infinite mercy. Here, then, if we may use human language, was the divine dilemma. How could he pardon the sinner without compromising his justice? How could he judge the sinner without frustrating his love? How in the face of human sin could he be at the same time a God of love and of wrath? How could he both pardon the sinner and punish his sin? How could a righteous God forgive unrighteous men without involving himself in their unrighteousness.

God's solution

There was only one way. In his infinite justice he would exact the penalty for sin, but in his infinite mercy he would accept the penalty himself. Only thus could he express and satisfy both his love and his justice. So in the person of his Son Jesus Christ he entered the world which he had made. He identified himself with man in his need. In the womb of Mary his mother he took upon him our nature. On the cross of Calvary he took upon him our sins. He was first made flesh (John 1:14). He was then 'made sin' (2 Corinthians 5:21). In the silence and darkness of those terrible hours on the cross the sins of the whole world, of every place and of every generation, were laid on him.

One way in which two of the New Testament writers describe this by an Old Testament expression, namely, 'He bore our sins in his body' (1 Peter 2:24), and he was 'offered once to bear the sins of many' (Hebrews 9:28). What this means is that in his own innocent person he accepted the penalty and endured the consequences which our sins should have brought upon us.

Only Jesus Christ could have thus died for the sins of the world. Why? Because only he was Man, and sinless, and God. Because he was Man, he could represent Man, and bear the sins of men. Because he was sinless, he had no sins of his own for which atonement needed to be made. Because he was God, his life was of infinite value (so that it could be offered for the sins of all men), and of eternal worth (so that it could be offered for the sins of all time).

As, then, we look at the cross we cannot tell which is more apparent – the implacable antagonism of God towards sin, or the inextinguishable compassion of God towards the sinner. Both are fully satisfied at the cross.

God has done everything that was necessary for our salvation. What then is there left for us to do? Nothing – but to acknowledge our sin, turn from it, and receive Jesus Christ into our life as our Saviour, committing ourselves personally to him, and asking God for Christ's sake to take our sins away.

J. R. W. Stott

10
Did Jesus really rise from the dead?

To answer this question it is necessary to be sure in the first place whether he was really dead, and in the second place whether he was genuinely and uniquely alive again afterwards. Accounts of people being raised from the dead are found elsewhere in the Bible, including three by Jesus himself, but in each case they returned to life in a way exactly similar to that of their former life, and had subsequently died. They were resuscitated rather than resurrected.

The biblical claim is that Jesus was fully human not only in his life on earth, but also in the fact that he died a physical death, that he did 'taste death for every man' (Hebrews 2:9 *Phillips*), and that he became alive again by a unique and miraculous event which left him with a body that made him, in a sense, more alive than those miraculously raised from the dead before, a body freed from many physical limitations, and which, above all, was not subject to illness or death, although it bore the scars of wounds inflicted in his earthly life. This was a 'first,' a unique event. He was 'the first fruits of those who have fallen asleep' (1 Corinthians 15:20).

Was he really dead?
If Jesus was not in fact physically dead (*ie* dead in the ordinary, everyday medical sense), there are several possible explanations of what subsequently happened, although there is no evidence whatever to enable us to assess their various values. We may dismiss the phenomenon of catalepsy, an exceedingly rare condition in which the subject is in a coma and appears to be dead, a condition discussed in a celebrated short story by Edgar Allan Poe in his *Tales of Mystery and*

Imagination, and savouring of the second of these two elements rather than the first!

Worthy of more serious consideration, at least on *prima facie* examination, is a suggestion made by an American doctor in 1908, that Jesus' apparent death was really a faint induced by the sufferings of the cross and that he subsequently recovered.

This idea has been revived recently by an anaesthetist (*Sunday Times*, 24 January 1965) who, in investigating the revival of patients after dental anaesthesia, found that some patients might be comatose for hours after anaesthesia, in the upright posture, though usually subsequently recovering. He postulated that the upright position of the body on the cross was similar to that of the patient in the dental chair, and that Jesus suffered from a cerebral anoxia which was not irreversible, and recovered in the tomb.

There are serious medical objections to such a view, and a professor of anaesthetics has in fact answered this proposal from a specialist point of view. The general medical objections are that even a fit young man, after several hours nailed to a cross in great heat, with infected lacerations of the hands and feet, and an open wound of the thorax made (no doubt far from gently) with a spear, placed in a cold tomb wrapped in heavy grave clothes, would be unlikely to survive unaided. The tomb was guarded, and his followers could not easily have fooled or overpowered the guards, and carried away their seriously-ill and badly-wounded leader.

In any case, the really serious objection here is a moral and theological one, rather than a medical and scientific one. There are, if this theory is correct, grave objections to the veracity of the whole New Testament account. Even worse, the Christianity which the apostles preached is based upon a lie. And what subsequently happened to Jesus? Did he go into hiding, live out his life in obscurity, condone the lies about him, being preached in his name? One thing is certain, it invalidates his repeated claim throughout his ministry that he was divine in as real a sense as he was human, that he was indeed the Son of God.

Was he really alive again?

Assuming that Jesus was in fact really dead, what are the possible alternatives to the New Testament claim that he rose again, that he was 'alive after his passion'? First, it has been suggested that those who purported to see him were the victims of an hallucination, partly because they were in a highly emotional state, partly because they wished and expected to see him alive again. It seems most unlikely that so many different individuals would all be victims of the same hallucination, or that some 500 people would all have the same hallucination at the same time (see 1 Corinthians 15:6). Besides this, the reality and objectivity of the events are borne out in the fact that Thomas could actually see and feel the wounds in his master's body.

In any case, it appears that the disciples were not *expecting* the resurrection. Peter and John were surprised and incredulous. The women at the tomb on the first Easter morning were dumbfounded. The disciples who walked with Jesus on the road to Emmaus were rebuked for their being 'slow of heart' (Luke 24:25 RSV).

Again, assuming that Jesus was in fact dead, it has been suggested that the body was stolen and concealed, either by his enemies (*ie* the Jewish authorities) or by his followers. The suggestion that the Jewish authorities (or the Roman administration, even) would wish to remove the body is an unlikely one. Such a device would open the door to the rumour of his resurrection, which is just what they would wish to prevent. A guard had been posted at the door of the tomb, and this, together with the fact that the 'door' was in fact a huge stone or rock, would have made it very difficult for the disciples to steal the body, even had they wished to. A group of frightened and dispirited men, such as they were, is hardly likely to have run the gauntlet of the guards. However, as with the suggestion that Jesus was not really dead, the objection to this theory is the serious moral and theological issue which it raises. If correct, it implies that the whole of Christianity is based upon a lie, because the existence of a risen, living and glorified Christ is an integral and essential part of New Testament Christianity. Not only would it lack this essential, but even the remaining moral teaching would be a mockery if its central premise were founded upon a cunning and contrived falsehood.

The only valid answer

This leads on to what is the only valid answer, namely, that Jesus was in fact 'alive after his passion.' This fits best with the documents and the facts. It alone can explain why and how the disciples, earlier defeated and broken as a group, became bold, confident, and successful in launching the infant church in a hostile world. They became men who preached Christ, crucified and risen. A concealed subterfuge, however successful as a deception, could not have brought this about: nothing but the conviction of the reality of the return of their lost leader, and the indwelling power of the Holy Spirit, after Pentecost; because if Jesus had still been dead, the giving of the Holy Spirit would have been impossible.

In the last analysis it is the testimony of countless Christians who have known 'him and the power of his resurrection' (Philippians 3:10) throughout 1900 years which looms largest as proof that Jesus rose from the dead and lives today as a risen Saviour. A teacher long since deceased, however good, however great, however inspiring, would have been no substitute.

A. P. Waterson

Can anyone today believe that Jesus 'ascended into heaven'?

At first sight this particular bit of the Apostles' Creed might seem to be about as far out of date as anything could be – an undoubtable casualty of the advance of scientific knowledge. Whatever else we may not know about the vast distances above our heads, we know now from actual experience that they are utterly devoid of the air and other necessities of human life, and (as some Russian friends have carefully pointed out) contain no visible traces of anything that might pass for 'heaven'. How then can we take seriously an article of faith that seems to teach the opposite?

The modern picture
But of course this question first raises another one. *Does* a belief that Christ 'ascended into heaven' mean a denial of these facts we have discovered, and of the model of the solar system we would all accept today? Granted that the Bible was written when men had a very different picture of the world, in terms of which (no doubt) people of the day would naturally interpret its teachings, is it the *purpose* of the Bible, or of the articles of faith based upon it, to teach or endorse that particular picture?

I think not. On the contrary, I suggest that although our twentieth century picture of the Universe may seem as queer and out of date in AD 4000 as the first-century picture does to us, nevertheless it is part of Christian duty to accept scientific discoveries thankfully as gifts from the same God who inspired the Bible writers, and that any idea of a conflict between them and what the Bible was *meant* to teach is out of the question.

What then are we, today, supposed to make of the story of Christ's ascension? Must we take it as a mere poetic invention, designed to teach an abstract lesson in a concrete way? I am no theologian; but I can see no *scientific* justification for rejecting the narrative as the honest recollection of credible witnesses to a unique event. To be sure, it was not the sort of event that a scientist (even a first century one) would have predicted; but then this was no ordinary man whose body is reported to have disappeared before the upward gaze of his disciples.

The mystery of the Ascension is presented to us as part and parcel of the mystery of the Resurrection, and of the whole Incarnation. It is but the last (and in a sense almost the inevitable) act in the mysterious drama of the appearance of the Creator himself as a human agent in his own creation, to live, to die, to triumph over death, and finally to return from the earthly scene to the glory that was eternally his. If this is really who Jesus was, it becomes no longer surprising that his life was attended by unprecedented events; the marvel is rather that they were relatively so few. Certainly no objection to their possibility could be raised from science, since science by its nature tells us only what we can expect 'according to precedent'. It can offer no sure guidance to our expectations of an occasion which is by definition unprecedented.

On the other hand, I think we must clearly distinguish between accepting as authoritative the *testimony* of these eye-witnesses, and accepting all the first century overtones of the *language* in which they expressed it. Failure to make this distinction has continually dogged the Church in its relations with science.[1] Divine inspiration of the gospel writers did not rob them of their normal mental furniture, and it would be mere false piety for us to look for *scientific* information in the terms they used. The right course, I am suggesting, will avoid both vague 'spiritualizing' on the one hand and crass literalism on the other.

Where did he go?
All right, one may say, but if Jesus did not literally take up a position in the sky over Palestine, where *did* he go? The answer of the Gospel of John is given in his own words: 'I am ascending to my Father and your Father' (John 20:17). Here, surely, is our clue; for the God of biblical theism is not described as located anywhere within his universe; it is rather the whole universe that has its being 'in him' (Acts 17:28).

From our earthly point of view, then, Christ's ascension was a disappearance, not just from one place to another but out of our space and time altogether. 'At the right hand of God,' he is now in touch not merely with one local part of his world, but with it all. Mysterious though it must be to us, we are assured that his human nature has not been abandoned in this transformation, so that there is real continuity between the Man who rose from the dead in Palestine and the One who is 'equal with the Father' in eternity. Doubtless it was in order to assure us of this continuity that, when the time came for his stay among us to end, he chose to vanish from sight by 'ascending up into heaven.' After all, what exit could have been more appropriate?

D. M. Mackay

1 For an excellent introduction to this topic see Professor R. Hooykaas, *Christian Faith and the Freedom of Science* (Tyndale Press) and *Religion and the Rise of Modern Science* (Scottish Academic Press).

12

Who or what is the Holy Spirit?

When Christians speak of the Holy Spirit they mean the life of Christ, the life of God himself indwelling and empowering, activating and transforming the people of God as individuals and as a body.

The purpose of God is to share with men his own life. The Son lived and died as a man in first-century Palestine so that men might be rescued from the power of sin and share in his life as God: this was his mission. But what the Son effected at a point in time, the Spirit was sent to extend and to make real and effective for men of every age. The life God gives through the Spirit to each believer is dynamic and forceful, and any tame notions of the Holy Spirit must give way to an understanding of him as God's power and presence among believers, the person who sums up all the strength and vitality of God.

The teaching of the Bible
The root meaning of the word for *spirit* in the Old Testament is *wind* or *breath* – not a breeze, but the powerful, sweeping desert wind; not a quiet, steady breathing, but agitated, violent breathing. Hence in the Old Testament *spirit* comes to denote the vital energy, the power of God. God created by his Word (Psalm 148:5), but by his Spirit he vitalized what he created (Psalm 104:30). However, though the Spirit as life-giver is basic in the Old Testament, he is more frequently mentioned as the source of the special gifts of men: *eg* of artistic skill (Exodus 36:1), of heroism in war (Judges 13:25, 14:6), of wisdom in government (1 Kings 3:28), and in particular as the source of the inspiration of the prophets, enabling them to speak boldly the mind of God (Numbers 11:29). But the activity of the Spirit in this sense can be described only in terms of irregular and spasmodic outbursts of

divine energy. The Spirit is not the constant possession of the people of God – the Spirit can depart from a man (1 Samuel 16:14; Psalm 51:11) – though there is the promise that this will not always be the pattern. To live as God designs he should live, man needs the life and power of God in fulness, and in this respect Ezekiel 36:26–27 is one of the climaxes of the Old Testament, for there the Spirit is promised as an abiding gift in connexion with the renewal of the covenant.

It is this promise which is fulfilled in the events of the New Testament. At his baptism, the Spirit is seen as remaining upon Jesus (John 1:32); his ministry is carried out in the power of the Spirit (Luke 4:1, 14, 18; Matthew 12:28); but it is only when Jesus has been glorified by his crucifixion, resurrection, and ascension, that the Holy Spirit can be given fully to abide among men (John 7:39). This 'setting free' of the Spirit was dependent on the completion of Jesus' work, but once set free the renewing and empowering work of the Spirit can be carried out universally. Pentecost (Acts 2) is the bestowing of the dynamic life of God through the Spirit on all who believe in Jesus, faith being the only prerequisite for receiving the Holy Spirit (John 7:38–39).

Pentecost

The importance of Pentecost lies in the permanent transformation of human life that began then as the redemption of Jesus is applied to men and his divine life given to them. The sensational features of that day (Acts 2:2–4) merely symbolize the inner power of the event and must not obscure the real significance of what happened.

Since Pentecost, the Spirit, which could in the Old Testament be interpreted as an impersonal force, had been demonstrated, in the most personal terms, to be the 'Spirit of Christ,' and so real was this in the experience of the New Testament writers that they refer to him as such (Romans 8:9; 1 Peter 1:11). Through his work men are brought into a personal relationship with Christ. His most distinctive task is to glorify Christ and to make him real (John 15:26, 16:14). The fruit of the Spirit (Galatians 5:22–23), which must develop in the Christian, are the qualities seen delineated in Christ. In fact to possess the Spirit is to possess Christ (Romans 8:9–10), and because the Spirit is the Spirit of Christ, he is known to be personal – he cannot be confused with any impersonal force, however dynamic.

The activity of the Spirit

But if the Spirit is the Spirit of Christ, what of his activity? All that the Old Testament said of the Spirit as life-giver and inspirer of the special gifts of men is maintained in the New Testament, but three particular aspects of his work are emphasized. First, that his activity in human life is inward. An individual is brought to new life by the Spirit (John 3:5–8), who thereafter in fulfilment of the promise of Ezekiel 36:27 resides in that life, causing not only a desire to walk in obedience to God, but the liberating power to do so (Romans 8:11). His indwelling work is one of transfiguration as he changes the believer into the likeness of the Lord (2 Corinthians 3:18), his work in this respect being one of the major themes of the New Testament.

As well as inward, the Spirit's activity is permanent: he is the permanent source of spiritual life and power, the permanent possession of the Christian believer. After Pentecost, Christians do not pray for the coming of the Spirit: they live in the Spirit.

They have not to call down an absent Spirit, but only to recall that they have once for all been received into a relationship with God, which means that they permanently have the Spirit in the depths of their being if not on the surface of their consciousness.
(A. R. Vidler)

Finally, the primary activity of the Spirit, in the New Testament, is to create the new community. It was when the disciples were together that the Spirit came upon them (Acts 2:1); it was he who welded them into a community, based on love, in which they held all things in common (Acts 2:44, 4:32); life in the Church, the body of Christ, is described as a sharing in the one Spirit (1 Corinthians 12:12–13); and the necessary gifts for building up the Church originate in the same Spirit (1 Corinthians 12:4–11). Indeed, the Church of the New Testament is 'the fellowship of the Spirit.' One of the modern heresies is to think of the Holy Spirit merely as an individual's possession. To receive the Spirit, according to the New Testament doctrine, means to be drawn out of isolation into that fellowship and common life of the Church, which is the prime sphere of the Holy Spirit's activity.

What is meant by the Holy Spirit? Nothing less than the life of God indwelling and empowering, activating and transforming the people of God, as individuals and as the body of Christ.

John A. Simpson

13

Should all Christians seek to speak in 'tongues'?

Expressions such as 'speaking in (other) tongues' come in two places in the Bible: in stories of the first Christians in Acts (2:1–21; 10:44–48; 19:1–7) and in Paul's first letter to the Christians at Corinth (1 Corinthians 12–14). Some other passages, such as the description of 'inarticulate groans' (Romans 8:26), may also refer to this experience.

Speaking in tongues meant speaking in words which you did not make up and did not understand (though you were in control of them). They were words you believed God gave you. They might be in some human language which others present could understand: in Acts 2 foreigners in Jerusalem recognized their own languages being spoken by the disciples, who were simple Galileans. Alternatively, they might not be understood by any human being, but only by God (1 Corinthians 14:2).

What was the point of a Christian speaking in tongues?

1 It could be a 'sign' that something supernatural had happened to you. It made clear to you and to other people that God was active in you. This use of tongues came at conversion or soon after. The passages in Acts describe this (see also 1 Corinthians 14:22).

2 It could be a way of building yourself up (1 Corinthians 14:4), perhaps of getting things off your chest, of giving expression to what your conscious mind found it difficult to come to terms with.

3 It could be a means of praying in the Spirit (1 Corinthians 14:14). When the praise of God deserves transcended human speech, then the language of angels might be more adequate. Again, there would be situations over which people agonized, when they just could not find words to use in praying for themselves or for others: then the Spirit would give them words (Romans 8:26–27).

4 It could be used in ministering to other people, the means of a message coming direct from God to them. This might be in the language of the hearer, though not of the speaker (see Acts 2); or it might be in some unintelligible language, in which case an interpreter was required (1 Corinthians 14:6–13).

One should not distinguish too sharply between these functions, as 1 Corinthians 14 again makes clear.

So should all Christians seek to speak in tongues? There are three main approaches to this question:

Some Christians believe that we should not seek to speak in tongues, because such spiritual gifts were only intended for New Testament times. See, for instance, Anthony Hoekema's book *What About Tongue Speaking?* (Paternoster). But the New Testament does not say that the gift is meant only for its own time, and indeed implies that such gifts will be needed until we 'see (God) face to face' (1 Corinthians 13:12). And it is difficult to believe that the actual experience of this gift which many Christians seem to have today is of demonic or purely psychological origin.

Some Christians believe that we may seek to speak in tongues, and that God does give this gift to many (for the uses referred to above). Some people who hold this view speak in tongues themselves; an example is Larry Christenson, who has written *Speaking in Tongues: A Gift for the Body of Christ* (Fountain Trust). Others who take this approach do not themselves speak in tongues, and this includes the present writer. I have explained this view in more detail in a booklet on 1 Corinthians 12–14, *The Church and the Gifts of the Spirit* (Grove Books).

Some Christians believe that we should all speak in tongues; Dennis and Rita Bennett in *The Holy Spirit and You* (Coverdale) take this view. But the New Testament does not, in my opinion, imply that all those who lack the gift of tongues are falling short of what God intends for them.

Those who stress the necessity of speaking in tongues commonly link it with being baptized in the Spirit. The New Testament assumes that all Christians will be baptized in the Spirit (see for instance

Matthew 28:19; 1 Corinthians 12:13). The question is, When does this baptism happen? Again there are several opinions:

Some Christians believe that baptism in the Spirit is part of what happens when you become a Christian: see, for instance, John Stott's booklet *The Baptism and Fullness of the Holy Spirit* (IVP). Certainly in the New Testament baptism and the giving of the Spirit are normally connected with conversion and being born again. But several passages in Acts describe people being baptized in the Spirit later than conversion, and many people today believe they have had this experience.

Some Christians believe that although baptism in the Spirit rightly belongs with conversion, in practice some people seem to miss out on the full reality of this, and thus God may give them (as he gave some people in Acts) a 'delayed honeymoon.' This latter phrase comes from the book *Did You Receive the Spirit?* by a Roman Catholic, Simon Tugwell (Darton, Longman, and Todd). I think this is a correct view, though again I have not had this experience myself.

Some Christians believe that everyone should have an experience of being baptized in the Spirit at some time later than their conversion. They believe baptism in the Spirit is separate from conversion. This view is put forward by the Bennetts in their book referred to above; but it does not appear to be consistent with the main teaching on baptism and the Spirit in the New Testament (see, for instance, Romans 6 and 8).

If the second view is the right one, then it indicates that God deals with different people in different ways. We need not feel troubled that we have not had the experience that other people have had; we cannot insist that others have the experience we have had; we need not deny the validity of the experience that others have had which we have not. The crucial question is not 'Have I been baptized in the Spirit, and, if so, when?' but 'Am I filled with the Spirit, dominated by the Spirit, *now?*'

Similarly Christians who speak in tongues will be wary of judging other Christians who do not. Further, they may need to beware of having only an emotional approach to faith in Christ – of not paying enough attention to the mind. And Christians who do not speak in tongues will be wary of judging or envying those who do. They will rejoice in what God has done for their brothers, and may seek this gift for themselves, but they will also recall that their being Christians at all is a wonderful evidence of the Spirit's work in their lives

(1 Corinthians 12:2). But they may need to beware of having only an intellectual approach to faith in Christ – of not paying enough attention to the spiritual side.

Both groups will avoid getting tongues out of proportion, and will seek gifts such as prophecy which are 'higher' because they involve the mind, and can be of more use in ministering to others and bringing people nearer Christ (see 1 Corinthians 14:1–15). In fact it is not important whether I have any particular gift: it is more important that I belong to a fellowship in which I can exercise my gift for the benefit of others and receive ministry from others with different gifts (see 1 Corinthians 14:26–40). But most important of all – more so than seeking of gifts – is the pursuit and practice of love (1 Corinthians 12:31; 13; 14:1).

John Goldingay

14

If there is only one God, how can we believe in God the Father, God the Son, & God the Holy Spirit?

One of the most important truths taught by the Bible is that there is only one God. It is scarcely too much to say that this is the outstanding lesson taught about God in the Old Testament. Because there is only one God, man's highest duty is to worship him alone, and the fount of all sin is to put anything or anyone else in his place or even on an equality with him. God stands in solitary and unapproachable pre-eminence. 'I am the Lord thy God: Thou shalt have none other gods but me' (the first of the Ten Commandments, Exodus 20:2–3, Prayer Book version).

This truth needs to be expressed even more strongly. It is not just that there is only one God, but that there *can* only be one God. This is because of what a 'god' is. Your 'god' is that which you put first, to which all else takes second place. But whatever men may put first in their lives, the Bible teaches that there is only One to whom that place belongs by right, the God who is the sovereign Lord and Creator of all things. He is First, Supreme above all, not because men make him so, but because he is. And therefore there can only be one God. You cannot have *two* things that are first, supreme above all, and to have more than one God is not merely wrong but impossible.

I am the Lord: that is my name;
my glory I not give to another.

(Isaiah 42:8)

I am the Lord, and there is no other, beside me there is no God.

(Isaiah 45:5)

Three persons

So there is only one God, the Father. What then are we to say of the Son and the Holy Spirit, whose divinity and equality with the Father

55

are everywhere presupposed in the New Testament? We say that they are three Persons but one God; the Father is God, the Son is God, and the Holy Spirit is God, but they are not three different Gods but the same God, for God is one.

This is the doctrine of the Trinity, and the evidence for it is simply the Bible evidence for the unity of God and for the divinity of the Son and the Spirit.

Alternative theories
There have not of course been lacking alternative explanations of the relation of the Son and the Spirit to the Father. There are only a limited number of ways in which this can be done, but they all fall down in reason and in Bible proof.

One person
One explanation is to deny that the Father, the Son and the Spirit are different persons. Instead they are merely three different guises under which the one God has successively appeared. This is the explanation of Swedenborgianism. The theory is absurd for it implies that God was not in heaven when he walked the earth in the guise of Christ; and it also does not square with Scripture.

It is quite clear in the New Testament that Father, Son and Spirit are three distinct persons, not one person playing different parts. Thus, at his baptism, Christ the Son stands in the River Jordan, the voice of the Father is heard in heaven, and the Spirit descends as a dove (Mark 1:10–11). Christ prayed to the Father that he would send the Spirit (John 14:16).

Three Gods
A more common explanation is simply to state bluntly that the Father, the Son and the Spirit are three Gods, not one. This is the explanation adopted by the Mormons, but of course it is a flat violation of the first commandment: 'Thou shalt have none other gods but me.' In spite of the real distinction between the three, many passages show that there is yet a oneness between them. Christians are baptized not 'in the names of the Father and of the Son and of the Holy Ghost,' but 'in the *name* . . .,' for they are *three* persons in *one* God. Again in John 14 Christ speaks of the coming of the Spirit (verses 16, 17) as involving the coming of himself also (verses 18, 21) and of the Father with him (verse 23). The presence of One in the heart is the presence of all Three. The only other explanation is to degrade the status of the Son and the Spirit.

Denying Christ's divinity

In the case of the Son this is sometimes done by saying that Christ was never God but only an elevated man who by virtue of his flawless moral life won to a unique degree adoption as God's Son. This is the teaching of Theosophy and Christadelphianism. Nevertheless the evidence in the Gospels for Christ's divinity is quite clear. So far from winning divine sonship by his life, Christ 'came from the Father' (John 16:28) in the first place, and the glory to which he returned at the end was simply 'the glory which I had with thee before the world was' (John 17:5).

The other way in which the status of Christ is degraded is by regarding him as a second-class god – god with a little *g*. This is the teaching of Jehovah's Witnesses. In spite of its apparent plausibility, it is at best a verbal quibble and at worst a violation of the first commandment. For the Bible knows of no sort of God worthy of the name except one who is first, supreme, and you cannot have a second-class first.

If Christ is not the same God as the Father, the only God, he is a being of so entirely different a character that to call him 'a god' is simply a misuse of words. Christ's teaching alone, however, rules out the idea of his being a god of a different order to the Father. 'I and the Father are one' (John 10:30). '... he who has seen me has seen the Father' (John 14:9). '... all should pay the same to the Son as to the Father' (John 5:23). Furthermore, statements referred to Jehovah in the Old Testament are often referred to Christ in the New.

Degrading the status of the Holy Spirit

The status of the Holy Spirit is commonly degraded by saying that he is not a person at all, but only the general 'influence' of God on men. This is the teaching of many sects, notably Christadelphians and Jehovah's Witnesses. But the Bible constantly speaks of the Holy Spirit as possessing mind, feeling and will of his own. He searches and knows (1 Corinthians 2:10–11); he can be grieved (Ephesians 4:30); he speaks and commands (Acts 13:2, 4, 16:6). Characteristics such as these can only be attributed to a distinct conscious person.

One God in three persons

We are left, then. with the conclusion that the Bible teaches that there is only one God; but his being is not a simple, transparent unity; within it there are the distinctions of Father, Son and Spirit. The Father is God, the Son is God, and the Holy Spirit is God; yet they are not three gods but they are all one God and the same God.

It ought not to surprise us that the character of God is more complex than we can readily understand. But the doctrine of the Trinity assures us that when we are saved by Christ and indwelt by the Spirit, we are not coming into contact with independent beings of an undefined status, but with him

who is the blessed and only Sovereign, the King of Kings, and Lord of Lords, who only has immortality, and dwells in unapproachable light; whom no man has ever seen or can see. (1 Timothy 6:15–16)

This was the unquestioning faith of the New Testament writers, and is still our faith today, to our inexpressible comfort.

J. K. Spence

15

Are we to take
the Bible teaching
about the
second coming of Jesus literally?

Anyone who reads the New Testament must be impressed with the frequent mention which is made of the expectation of Jesus Christ's return. In Jesus' teaching, the parables of the wise and foolish virgins (Matthew 25:1–13), and of the pounds (Luke 19:11–27) refer to himself as the one who comes, or who goes and comes again, while in more direct teaching (as in Matthew 24) there are frequent references to his coming again. The second coming of Christ was part of the early preaching of the Apostles as seen in the Acts, and was early incorporated into the sort of statements like 2 Timothy 4:1 which prepared the way for its becoming part of the earliest form of the Apostles' Creed by about AD 150. So it has remained, a part of the Christian confession of belief in Christ.

At the same time it must be recognized that some find this difficult to accept or to understand. Perhaps the problem may be stated in two different ways:

●Everything has gone on since the time of the New Testament, now nearly two thousand years. How long are we to go on believing that the hope of Jesus coming 'soon' is a real hope?

●The more we think of the universe in modern scientific terms, the more difficult it becomes to imagine or accept what the New Testament gives as a description of the second coming.

In other words, as the questions *when?* and *how?* are pressed, they raise in the minds of some the further question, *whether at all?* Now such a question could be simply answered by affirming the authority of Scripture as the Word of God which must be accepted; but this might well involve an unintelligent submission, which is not the kind of understanding faith which God requires from us, and which the Bible actually enables us to have.

When will he come?

Take the first problem. The New Testament itself mentions this as something that troubled the early Church.

> Where now is the promise of his coming? Our fathers have been laid to their rest, but still everything continues exactly as it has always been since the world began.
>
> (2 Peter 3:4 NEB)

Yet the answer was not that this hope was an outcome of early enthusiasm, now to be given up in the light of experience. The later writings like 2 Peter, or the epistles to Timothy and Titus, or the first epistle of John and John's Gospel, all continue to hold out this hope (*eg* 2 Timothy 4:1; 1 John 2:28; John 5:28, 14:3). It was a hope that was not fulfilled by the coming of the Holy Spirit at Pentecost, nor by death, nor by 'comings' in present judgments. While in various ways these are linked to the second coming of Christ, they do not replace it; they prepare for and point forward to it. Above all, as John 5:24–29 teaches, the present hearing of Christ's voice to receive the gift of eternal life anticipates the final hearing of his voice when he returns; the present 'coming' to the life of the believer prepares for the final coming of the Lord to receive his own.

But time marches on. Yet the answer to this difficulty is given in the passage from 2 Peter quoted above. First of all, to put it into proper perspective, it is important to remember who God is. He is the creator of the whole universe, and its judge (2 Peter 3:5–7). He is the Lord of time and of our human history, and he has a purpose in that history about which he makes promises and predictions (vv. 8–9, *cf* verse 2). Involved in his historical purpose is his work of salvation by which the sinner is brought to repentance. This view of history agrees with Christ's teaching (*eg* Matthew 24) that there will be all kinds of national upheavals, the sort of thing history is made up of, and within that 'this gospel of the kingdom will be proclaimed throughout the earth as a testimony to all nations; and then the end will come.' In other words the mission of the Church, guided by the Holy Spirit, is part of the work of God's mercy to all men so that none shall perish. Its testimony to all nations is part of the preparation for the second coming. It is not surprising therefore that in 2 Peter 3, Christians are urged to 'hasten on' the Day of God.

How will he come?

Accepting then that this time-lapse presents no great difficulty if seen in this way, how are we to imagine this momentous event? In some ways this problem cannot be answered except by the coming itself. We need to remember that the events of Christ's first coming were not as people had expected, even though he came among people who were well read in the promises and prophecies of his coming.

Indeed it is clear that many resisted the knowledge they had, and refused to see the Old Testament prophecies fulfilled in Christ. Yet God strangely and wonderfully worked out his purpose even though few realized what was going on. During Christ's life the mistaken expectation of a military Messiah confused people's thinking. And how few, even of the prepared disciples, realized that on the cross God's great work of redemption was being completed.

In the same way this final coming of Christ will take many by surprise, as the New Testament repeatedly warns us. Normal life will be going on: 'there will be marrying and giving in marriage' (*cf* Matthew 24:37–41), so that it will be quite possible for the event to steal up on people 'like a thief.' Throughout the New Testament, however, there is warning that it will be at a time when, on the one hand, there will be flagrant and open opposition to the truth and worship of God, with an impressive regime of evil. On the other hand, men will be afraid, even though they assure themselves of security; and this fear will affect many religiously minded folk so that they lapse from true devotion to God.

This entire 'event,' as it brings history to an end, is described in the New Testament in terms of a fiery destruction, which affects not only mankind but the physical universe (2 Peter 3:7, 10; 1 Corinthians 3:13). Some may think of this as 'pictorial,' but it must have a meaning, and quite clearly that meaning is destruction, although with a view to re-creation. It needs to be remembered, however, that while it is quite true that the New Testament does speak in pictures and symbols, it does this in writing where this is consciously used as a literary form. It is not apparent that in the epistles we can take it that this is so without clear indication. Further, it is certain that the circumstances of Christ's first coming were foretold and fulfilled, in some cases to the letter.

In this matter of the final end when Christ returns, the literal possibility of these circumstances being fulfilled is not outside the bounds. The terrible possibilities of nuclear fission cannot be ignored. As Archbishop Lord Fisher once hinted, it would not be contrary to the working of divine providence for God's plan for the completion of history to be brought about through man's sinful pride unleashing upon himself the final judgment in terms of uncontrollable destructiveness which exceeded his own vaunted scientific knowledge.

Christ's testimony

This is where we begin to speculate. To return to clear certainty, we can see that the sure testimony of Christ himself to his return makes sense of the whole purpose of God. It presents to us the assurance that God's victorious purpose to restore sinful creation to his original purpose is going to be fulfilled in his time. At the moment, Christ's victory through the cross and his reign is still challenged; but not for always. Full salvation and final restoration, the forces of evil completely dealt with, is God's promise and will. This, with all that is involved, is the Christian's hope, and it is centred in the full and final revelation of his Lord.

George Marchant

16

What do we know about heaven & the future life?

How will Roman Catholics be happy in heaven if they can't play bingo? The questioner in the railway compartment was quite serious. His travelling companion replied that everything in heaven will be so new and wonderful that earthly pleasures will be altogether transcended. Was he right? Or was it just wishful thinking? Isn't the whole idea of heaven as a place where everyone will be completely happy a gigantic piece of self-deception? Isn't it an attempt to balance up the injustices and inequalities of this present life with an imaginary state of bliss beyond the stars? 'Pie in the sky when you die' as the saying goes?

The objection seems fair enough if you think of heaven merely as a future state. For then it becomes so remote and tenuous that a distant corner of interstellar space would appear to be the only suitable location for it. But heaven can begin here and now. It can be literally 'down our street.' Let me explain.

Heaven here and now

Quite simply, heaven is where God is. And God is everywhere. More particularly is he in the hearts of those who love him. To receive Christ as Saviour is to enter into a new relationship with God: 'the old order has gone, and a new order has already begun' (2 Corinthians 5:17 NEB). This new order is what we mean by 'heaven': the place where God is known and loved and served. Not a geographical or spatial location but a relationship which can be ours this present moment. So the old lady was right when in response to the question 'Can you prove to me that there is such a place as heaven?' she replied 'Yes! I live there.' For everyone who believes in Christ 'has already passed from death to life' (John 5:24 NEB), and 'has eternal life' (John 3:36 RSV).

Our 'future life' therefore is not entirely disconnected from our present life as Christians. It is a prolonging and intensification of what we have already begun to experience in Christ. What we call 'death' is but a moment in a developing experience, a moment when we enter into a fuller realization of Christ's presence and power.

The Holy Spirit
Meanwhile we have the gift of the Holy Spirit as a 'first instalment' of our inheritance. He is the 'pledge of what is to come' (2 Corinthians 1:22 NEB). Already through the Spirit we enjoy the privileges of the kingdom, already 'with angels and archangels and with all the company of heaven' we take our place in the celestial choir, praising and thanking and serving God for ever.

At the same time the world is still very much with us, with all its suffering and sin, its frustrations and temptations. 'For now we see through a glass, darkly; but then face to face' (1 Corinthians 13:12). Spiritual realities are but dimly glimpsed, and it is only in moments of special exaltation that we become aware of our true citizenship (see Philippians 3:20 RV). At death we believe all these limitations will be removed. For 'What no eye has seen, nor ear heard, nor the heart of man conceived ... God has prepared for those who love him' (1 Corinthians 2:9 RSV).

Beyond Death
In the Bible – more especially in the Book of Revelation – the representation of what awaits us beyond death is given in symbolic language. We read of harps and ceaseless songs of praise, of palms and crowns and flowing robes of white. These things are not meant to be taken literally. They express the ideas of joy and fulfilment which will be characteristic of the life hereafter. But, as we have seen, these are qualities of life which we can taste already. Here then is our proof of their reality.

The qualities of life which are ours in Christ cannot be contained within this earthly scene. They belong to him who is eternal. Death did not mean the end of *his* existence. No more will it mean the end of ours. In so far as we are 'in Christ' we have passed with him from death to life and are already walking in the courts of heaven. What we call 'death' will bring an enlargement of the potentialities which are ours in him.

But just where is all this development going to take place? In this world or in some new environment? Some Scriptures imply a transformation of this present universe; others speak of an entirely new heaven and new earth. One may be a preliminary stage to the other. The post-resurrection appearances of our Lord show us that we shall still have physical bodies, but they will be free from the limitations which are imposed upon them here. And they will be free from sin. This after all may be the norm of human existence, human existence as God meant it to be. As it is, we have got so used to the idea of sin and suffering and death that we find it difficult to conceive of human life without these concomitants. But man's spirit yearns for something better. All down the ages men have envisaged a state of affairs when they will be free from frustration and fear. In our own times man is trying harder and harder to reproduce these ideal conditions which have haunted him so long. Easy communications, bodily well-being and longevity, power over nature, space-travel – what are these but brave attempts to achieve a heaven of his own making? Is he to be mocked for ever? Is there no way towards an attainment of his dreams?

We believe there is. Not by his own unaided effort but by God's own gift of new, unquenchable life will man be able to enjoy the purpose for which God created him. And that will be heaven.

Leo Stephens-Hodge

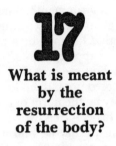

What is meant by the resurrection of the body?

Some of the earliest Christians found it hard to believe in a future resurrection, and hard to conceive of what the resurrection of the body could mean. In one long chapter of the New Testament, namely I Corinthians 15, Paul honestly discusses their difficulties.

So in this key chapter we find not just 'teaching' on the subject, but answers to real questions. They are questions which people still ask today, and indeed they have special point in the present age of science and materialism.

Do we possess any observable parallels to resurrection in ordinary everyday life?

One obvious starting-point which the Bible takes up is the everyday experience of waking up in the morning. The dreams of the night fade away, and we re-orientate ourselves to the reality of the new day with all its promise.

But the Bible especially uses parallels from nature, and these help us at three points.

First, they can help us to imagine how strikingly *different* the new resurrection body will be from the physical body which we discard at death. The difference will be at least as striking as the difference between a flower or fruit and the seed from which it grew. When we bury a seed in the earth, we do not expect it later to rise up out of the ground in its original form! Similarly, when we bury the body of flesh and bones we do not expect it to rise at the resurrection in anything much like its original form (1 Corinthians 15:35–38). (Incidentally, this is why we cannot object to cremation solely on the grounds of the resurrection of the 'body'.)

But secondly, parallels from nature can help us to appreciate how we shall still retain our *recognizable identity* even in the resurrection body. When we buy a tulip bulb from a nurseryman, he can usually tell us whether it will come up as a black one or as a red and yellow one. Each bulb retains its identity through all its process of change, and when at last we have a bed of tulips, we can recognize each one from the descriptions which came with the bulbs. In just the same way, even through the mysterious process of transformation into a new existence, we shall remain 'ourselves,' and be recognizable as such.

Thirdly, the heart of the resurrection experience will be *transformation*. We find hints of the idea not only in the realm of plant-life. One day an ugly little grub turns into a dragonfly or a caterpillar turns into a glorious butterfly. The transformation enables it to live in a new world. Resurrection, too, involves transformation; but not just transformation from the physical. The transformation extends to the realm of values.

Nature gives us glimpses even into this idea. Whatever could a caterpillar know or appreciate about flying? Or a tadpole about breathing air? Whatever, then, could an earth-conditioned human know or appreciate about the beauty of God? But one day transformation will come; and then experience and knowledge will match it.

If the resurrection body is not strictly 'physical' at all, what do we mean by the word 'body'?

The Bible sharply distinguishes between the resurrection of the body and the idea of the immortality of the soul.

The point of the distinction is this: Christians believe that resurrection life will be richer, deeper, and fuller than life in the physical body; that it will be *more but not less* than physical life. In contrast to this rich new experience, the Old Testament describes the bare survival of the soul in pathetic terms, rather like the dreary existence of a semi-conscious ghost! For the 'body' is what enables us to *live*, and not just to survive. The more sensitive our palate, for instance, the more we can enjoy our food. The more efficient our ears, the more deeply we can enjoy music, and so on.

But this does not mean that an efficient 'body' has to be a physical body. We may be tempted to assume this, but only because physical or material bodies are the only kind we have so far known. Of course an efficient body has to be a physical body *given the conditions of our own universe*. But no one can seriously imagine that we shall make heavenly music by means of vibrating sound waves. At the same time, we *shall* be able to enjoy deeper, richer, non-physical *counterparts* to music. Otherwise much of the symbolism of the Book of Revelation would be pointless. This is why it remains helpful, and not contradictory, to speak of the resurrection of the body.

How can we believe what we cannot even imagine?

The Bible restates the problem of belief in the future resurrection as a matter of belief in the omnipotence of God.

Once again 1 Corinthians 15 appeals to the analogies of creation. Look at the problems of manufacture and design which God has overcome already. Whatever new environment God has thought of for his creatures, he has found precisely the appropriate 'body' for them: feathers and wings for creatures in the sky, burning gases for outer space, and by the same token, resurrection 'bodies' for eternity.

How can we best anchor against guesswork or wishful thinking?

The Bible anchors all its discussion about the resurrection of Christians in the resurrection of Jesus Christ. But it says very little about the resurrection of others, except for two terrifying statements, that some will experience a resurrection into a condition of condemnation and disgrace (Daniel 12:2; John 5:29). The possession of a 'body' would mean that the unpleasantness of such an experience would be felt at least as keenly as ever it could have been in the full consciousness of this present life.

In the case of Christians, however, Paul describes our Lord's resurrection as the 'first-fruits', or sample, of what they will one day experience (1 Corinthians 15:20, 23).

We can anchor confidently in this fact, as long as we bear one point in mind; we know only about the forms which our Lord's risen body took when he appeared to those who were still living within the conditions of our own universe. The Gospels tell us about *some* of the forms which his body could take, but not about all of them. We should hardly expect that the full splendour of his heavenly glory *could* have been communicated to disciples who still saw him only with earthly eyes.

What we do know, however, confirms exactly what we noted about the word 'body'. Our Lord's risen body was certainly *more* than physical; for instance, it could pass through closed doors. But it was not *less* than physical, because the risen Christ could still enjoy the fine taste of freshly-caught fish, and Thomas could still identify him as the One on whom the soldiers had inflicted a spear wound.

In one more respect, as well as in all these, the risen bodies of Christians will be like that of their Lord's. Their new bodies will no longer act as vehicles for self-interest. They will express to the full the wonder, the adoration, and the radiant contentment, of those who will be enjoying the immediate presence of God. All the dishonourable associations of the old physical body will have been forgotten. God will raise it in glory and triumphant power (1 Corinthians 15:43, 49–58).

Anthony C. Thiselton

18

Isn't the wrath of God at variance with his love?

One good way of understanding this is to look at Jesus, who reveals the character of God to us. Of Jesus' love for men there can be no question: his death on the cross was proof of that. But his love was never sentimental. It had a stern side to it when he met with the sham religion of his day and the sin of men.

The example of Christ

His love for those in need was wounded and affronted when he healed a man with a withered hand and the churchgoers of the day resented this being done on the sabbath.

He said to them, 'Is it lawful on the sabbath to do good or to do harm, to save life or to kill?' But they were silent. And he looked around at them with anger, grieved at their hardness of heart. (Mark 3:4–5)

Anger or wrath was as much a part of Jesus' character as love. It is best thought of as the righteous reaction of a sinless person, expressed as moral indignation at the hard-heartedness of men. Jesus hated the pious play-acting which passed for religion in his day and he denounced it vigorously. His title for the religious leaders, 'hypocrites,' shows this same moral indignation. The most striking example of the wrath of Jesus in the Gospels is the incident in the temple, where he found traders making money out of the needs of the pilgrims. Many of these latter were poor people who could barely afford the price of the sacrifices which were prescribed, but this had not prevented traders from turning the system into a shameless profit-making concern. To see the house of God put to this debased use and to see the poor exploited in this way roused Jesus to deep moral indignation. Taking a whip of cords and advancing on the scene of oriental bartering, he drove out the traders and their animals and overturned their tables and money counters. Here is a dramatic picture of wrath in action: Jesus reacts against the sinful practice and then carries out his judgment in cleansing the temple.

God's action against sin

The wrath of God is to be thought of then as his righteous anger at human sin and his action against it. The Bible shows him to be 'holy,' separated from and uncontaminated by sin. He cannot tolerate sin in his presence and he is 'of purer eyes than to behold evil' and 'cannot look on wrong' (Habakkuk 1:13). As the 'Judge of all the earth' (Genesis 18:25) he will not stand by as a sort of casual spectator while wrong is done. On the contrary, he is determined to see justice done and evil punished.

You shall not afflict any widow or orphan. If you do afflict them, and they cry out to me, I will surely hear their cry; and my wrath will burn.   (Exodus 22:22–24)

Men think that they can 'get away with it'; but the Bible is clear that although God may exercise great patience with sinners, he does not condone sin and there will be a time when this will be seen to be so.

St Paul, confronted by the open immorality in the pagan world of his day, wrote to people who thought like this:

Do you suppose, O man, that when you judge those who do such things and yet do them yourself, you will escape the judgment of God? Or do you presume upon the riches of his kindness and forbearance and patience? Do you not know that God's kindness is meant to lead you to repentance? But by your hard and impenitent heart you are storing up wrath for yourself on the day of wrath when God's righteous judgment will be revealed.   (Romans 2:3–5)

Christ's teaching

Nor can we brush this off as the teaching of St Paul alone and not of Jesus. As well as showing the reality of wrath in his own life, Jesus taught about the stern side of God's character and his judgment:

... do not fear those who kill the body but cannot kill the soul; rather fear him who can destroy both soul and body in hell.   (Matthew 10:28)

He likened God to a master who forgave a servant a huge debt, only to find the same servant demanding money with violence from another man who owed him a trifling sum. Note the master's reaction:

Then his lord ... said to him, 'You wicked servant! I forgave you all that debt because you besought me; and should not you have had mercy on your fellow servant, as I had mercy on you?' And in anger his lord delivered him to the jailers.
(Matthew 18:32–34)

Here is a vivid picture of what happens when we abuse God's forgiveness by not forgiving others. We incur his wrath, his righteous indignation. This stern and severe aspect of God is as much a part of the Bible's picture of him as is his love. In fact, it is *because* God loves so deeply that he is moved to anger by the hardness of men. Jesus' anger is aroused by the hard and unfeeling attitude of those who resent his love shown in healing the man with the withered hand. It is to the people on whom he had showered his love that God says: 'You only have I known of all the families of the earth; therefore I will punish you for all your iniquities' (Amos 3:2). Like a father, he cannot tolerate the sin which ruins his children, and his anger is directed against it. His wrath is the expression of his love confronted by evil which wounds it. In part his wrath is already known whenever men reject his love and they already reap terrible consequences (Romans 1:18); but his wrath will not be finally known until the judgment day which all men will face.

T. E. Yates

19
Hell...
fact or fiction?

If our Christian convictions resulted from our desires or wishful thinking there would be few who believe in hell. Who could wish such an awful fate for any of their fellow men?

But, nonetheless, the conviction persists in the Church that what we are redeemed from is just such a destiny. The reasons behind this conviction must be very strong, for who has not felt the force of the many objections so often made against the whole idea of eternal punishment? I will examine some of these objections.

Christ's teaching

First, it is said that Jesus never really taught the fact of hell. A correspondent to a church paper, applauding an article calling for the dismissal of the 'vulgar superstition' of hell wrote, 'So very often the so-called teaching of Christianity is founded on the Old Testament, St Paul, and the early fathers and the Reformers, instead of on Jesus of Galilee.' C. S. Lewis had some forthright things to say about this sort of statement in his preface to J. B. Phillips' *Letters to Young Churches*; but we can check such an astonishing misconception in twenty minutes by reading straight through one of the Gospels. The following selection from Matthew's Gospel is worth serious study, not least the quotations from the Sermon on the Mount: Matthew 5:21 *ff*; 29 *ff*; 7:13, 23; 8:12; 10:15, 28, 39; 11:24; 12:32; 13:40 *ff*, 49a; 16:24 *ff*; 18:6–9, 14; 22:11–14; 23:13 *ff*; 24:36 *ff*; 25:12, 30, 41; 26:24.

The aim and nature of punishment

Secondly, it is said that punishment which does not end in reform is valueless. This argument is popular today, but constant repetition does not make it less misleading. Of course, in our administration of justice, we rightly endeavour to reform all offenders. But this is not always possible; some will not be reformed. Does that mean that such are to be set free directly we realize that they are incorrigible? No, those who break the laws of society deserve to be punished whether or not the punishment in question reforms them, or deters others, in the process. A few moments' thought will show that an acceptance of the concept of retribution is essential if justice is to be done.

Another objection to the New Testament warnings on hell is that eternal punishment for sins committed during a short life would be unreasonable. The real trouble with this kind of statement is that the stress upon length of time only muddles the issue. But we would be most unwise to interpret the word 'eternal' in terms of one year after another. When Jesus is said to have purchased for us eternal redemption, the meaning is 'redemption with an eternal result.' So, eternal life or death is life or death with an eternal result, *ie* an irrevocable verdict. This is to say that the familiar hope for a 'second chance' after this life is illusory (the point is illustrated in Luke 16:26). This world and this life are the place and time where destinies are decided and the direction of life determined.

But the real misunderstanding here concerns not the number of our sins but the nature of them. The Bible teaches that our sins (what we do) are comparatively trivial compared with our sin (what we are). Our sin is that we have chosen to live in God's world without him, and to direct our lives according to our own will. What we are condemned for is that we have been offered light but prefer darkness (John 3:17–21). The whole Bible story concerns God's activity through Christ to bring back his prodigal creation. But nothing can alter the miserable fact that so many resist to the last his offers of redemption. Any minister of the gospel can testify to the fact that the proud heart of man is determined to keep its independence. What do we want God to do with such? To leave them alone? It seems that this is indeed their dreadful punishment (Matthew 7:23).

Hell and God's love
In the last resort the only serious objection to the idea of hell is that the love of God absolutely forbids such an idea. I think it fair to say that many Christians today incline to Universalism. God's love, they feel, must ultimately prove victorious over all. But if the problem of hell is to be resolved like this, how could the New Testament writers report both the marvellous teaching of Jesus about God's Father-hood, and the awesome teaching of the certainty of hell for the

impenitent, without an intolerable sense of contradiction? Beyond question, the New Testament writings include the strongest possible emphasis both on the love and on the severity of God. There is no hint that the one ultimately excludes the other.

On the contrary, it should be said that it was the absolute certainty in the apostles' minds that God could not condone man's rebellion that made them so unshakeably sure that God is love! They saw that God could by no means clear the guilty; they recognized that they were guilty and yet beloved; and then to their amazed wonder they saw that, rather than let them bear the penalty of their own sin, God had sent his Son into the world to become Man to bear the fearful penalty in their place and in their stead. It was because they were so certain of God's 'wrath and indignation against us' that they were so sure of his unquenchable love towards us. So great was this love that he actually accepted in the person of Christ his own sentence of death (see 1 John 4:10 and note that a propitiatory sacrifice, so far from being unnecessary because of God's love, was in fact its supreme demonstration and proof).

But there is a further point here of immense importance. God's love can never be irresistible. The apparent difficulty of squaring the Creator's love for his creatures with the possibility of their ultimate condemnation arises only when we ignore the real measure of human responsibility each man possesses. God has offered a completely new beginning to all men through Christ. But suppose – astonishing folly! – we will not accept that offer? God promises abundant mercy to the penitent. But suppose we will not repent? What then will God do? Will he remove from us the ability to say no to him? But that would be to make us less than human beings.

'Happily ever after'?

When all is said and done, what becomes of the whole Christian faith if hell is found to be fictitious? Then we must say that the biblical warnings about the danger and destructiveness of sin are thoroughly exaggerated and morbid. Then we must say that the agonizing sufferings of Christ – truly hell on earth – were shockingly unnecessary. Then we must say the choice between life and death with which the whole Bible confronts us is a colossal bluff.

Perhaps one of our troubles today is that to many people the Bible is like the other story books of their childhood where, whatever else happened, you could be sure that in the end everyone would live happily ever after. Is not this how its message is sometimes presented? But the Bible is not a fairy story, and the truths and choices it presents are not make-believe. It is better to let no man deceive us with empty words.

Be sure of this, that no immoral or impure man, or one who is covetous (that is, an idolator), has any inheritance in the kingdom of Christ and of God.

(Ephesians 5:5)

Until this warning is sounded once again, clearly as well as compassionately, in our presentation of the Faith, we are unlikely to see any great awakening in the ranks of paganism.

Dick Lucas

20

Is there really a coming day of judgment?

Christians are sometimes accused of being so heavenly minded that they are no earthly good. But as often as not, the truth is just the opposite. We are so earthly minded that we are no heavenly good. And the Christian who is no heavenly good is not likely to be much earthly good either.

The teaching of Christ

This is a point Jesus often made. His teaching was always concerned to put life in its proper perspective. Time after time he impressed upon his hearers that this life is not the end, that there will come a time when we shall all have to give account of ourselves and be judged accordingly. What is more, he was equally emphatic that he himself would be the judge and the judgment would be final and irrevocable.

All this is unmistakably clear if we study such passages as Matthew 7:13–27, 10:26–33, 12:36 f, 13:24–49, 22:1–14, 24:1–25, 46; Mark 8:34–38, 13:1–37; Luke 12:1–59, 13:23–30, 16:19–31; John 5:22–29, 6:39. It is not so much a matter of threatening people into morality, but of reminding them that what we do here and now has eternal significance. And *vice versa*. Our view of eternity should make a great deal of difference to what we do here and now.

No one can prove that there will be a judgment day. Neither does anyone know when it will be. Jesus himself admitted that he did not know (Mark 13:32). But he did say that it would come when people would least expect it. Christians believe that there will be a judgment on the authority of Jesus and the revelation given to the prophets and apostles. It is like accepting the word of an ambassador on the basis of his credentials. Because his credentials give him authority to speak, we can accept his word on the subject on which he is commissioned to speak. But there is also another point to consider. God would hardly be God if he turned a blind eye upon everything that went on in the world. If God is just and holy, it is impossible not to believe in a day of reckoning. In fact, the real problem is not persuading ourselves that there will be a day of judgment, but seeing how anyone could face Almighty God at all on that day.

Christians and judgment

The Bible is unambiguously clear that no one can save himself. We have all repeatedly flaunted God's goodness and broken his laws. This applies not only to what we have done or failed to do, but to what we have said and thought (Matthew 5:27–30). But God so loved men that he sent his Son to take the consequences of our sin and die in our place (Matthew 26:28; Mark 10:45; John 1:29, 3:16; Romans 3:23–25; 2 Corinthians 5:14–21; Galatians 3:10–13; 1 John 2:2). Those who run to him in faith find forgiveness and full acceptance with God (Matthew 11:27–30; John 3:16–18, 5:24; Romans 1:16 *f*; 1 John 1:9).

But a question Christians sometimes ask is this: if this is so, will Christians still have to face the judgment? We can see how Jesus and Paul would have answered this if we look at the parables of the talents and the sheep and goats (Matthew 25:14–46) and such passages as Romans 14:10, 1 Corinthians 3:10–15, and 2 Corinthians 5:10. All who have found forgiveness in Christ are assured that he will not turn them away. Nevertheless, their lives will be scrutinized. Some will even be rewarded. But the work of others will fail to pass the test and be destroyed, even though they themselves will be saved.

Judgment in this life

This brings us back to the point at which we began. There is a very real sense in which judgment will bring everything to light and confirm the final verdict. But it is what we do here and now that decides the final issue. And the basic factor will be whether we have taken up the offer of forgiveness in Christ. As Jesus said,

Truly, truly, I say to you, he who hears my word and believes him who sent me, has eternal life; he does not come into judgment, but has passed from death to life.
(John 5:24)

He who believes in him is not condemned; he who does not believe is condemned already because he has not believed in the name of the only Son of God.
(John 3:18)

In looking at this question we have looked mainly at the teaching of

Jesus on judgment. But the theme runs right through scripture. For further study see the teaching of the prophets on *the day of the Lord* in the Old Testament. Among the important passages in the New Testament on the last things are the following: Romans 8–11, 1 Corinthians 15, 1 and 2 Thessalonians, Hebrews, 2 Peter, and the Book of Revelation.

Colin Brown

21

What about
the people who
lived before
Christ came?

Before we answer this question, there are some preliminary general considerations to be noted, so that we may answer the question against its true setting.

Preliminary considerations

God's will. Not once but many times in Scripture it is made clear that it is not God's 'will for any to be lost but that all should come to repentance' (2 Peter 3:9). Therefore it is clear that he would wish those people who were on earth *in time* before Christ not to be left out.

Human time and God's time. We count time in man-made minutes, hours, and days, and with us there is a 'before' and 'after' in time. This is not necessarily true of God, as Peter comments: 'with the Lord one day is like a thousand years, and a thousand years like one day' (2 Peter 3:8). How else could Christ's sacrifice almost 2,000 years ago apply to me and my redemption today, for I was unborn when Christ died for *my* sins? And if it seems unreasonable that *God* should 'annihilate' time, let us remember in this space age that *man* has 'annihilated' space, both by television and by rocket. Cannot then Christ's sacrifice apply both *forwards* in time, and *backwards* in time?

Salvation is of universal application. John tells us that the Lord Jesus 'is the expiation for our sins, and not for ours only, but also for the sins of the whole world' (1 John 2:2 RSV). And Jesus himself said: 'All that the Father gives me will come to me, and the man who comes to me I will never turn away' (John 6:37).

Those who died before Christ

With these three points in mind, let us now consider those who died before Christ came. There is very little direct evidence in Scripture concerning them, but there are many passages in the New Testament which comment favourably upon the Old Testament heroes of faith, notably Hebrews 11. In its last two verses we read:

These also, one and all, are commemorated for their faith; and yet they did not enter upon the promised inheritance, because with us in mind, God had made a better plan, that only in company with us should they reach their perfection.

So from the passage it is clear that Old Testament and New Testament believers are bound up together in Christ. Remember that Christ himself said, 'Before Abraham *was*, I *AM*,' (John 8:58 AV). Man is finite, Christ is infinite. Two verses earlier Jesus said, 'Your Father Abraham was overjoyed to see my day; he saw it and was glad.' The first fifteen verses of John 1 also apply.

Paul's particular approach to the Gentiles in regard to conscience in Romans 1 and 2, notably Romans 1:20, has a bearing on this. 'His invisible attributes, that is to say his everlasting power and deity, have been visible, ever since the world began, to the eye of reason, in the things he has made. There is therefore no possible defence for their conduct.'

The apostle Peter tells us of Christ that

In the body he was put to death; in the spirit he was brought to life. And in the spirit he went and made his proclamation to the imprisoned spirits. They had refused obedience long ago. (1 Peter 8:18–20)

The interpretation of this passage is, of course, debatable, but it has been argued from the earliest Christian days that during the time that the body of Jesus lay in the tomb, his spirit was proclaiming his atoning death and his forthcoming resurrection to all those who had 'died before Christ', so that they should not be left out of the promise which applied to all men since.

What is the 'prison'? Surely, simple *hades* – the place of departed spirits is meant. When Christ died upon the cross, he said to the dying thief, 'Today you shall be with me in Paradise' (Luke 23:43). The Creed says, 'He descended into hell'; but our English word *hell* translates two different Greek words. It covers both *gehenna*, the place of divine judgment, and *hades* (the word used in the Creed), the place of departed spirits. Note that the 'you' and the 'me' of Luke 23:43 make it clear that our identity is not lost in the future life.

A further comment which comes from Peter, says,

Why was the Gospel preached to those who are dead? In order that, although in the body they received the sentence common to men, they might in the spirit be alive with the life of God. (1 Peter 4:6)

This is not exhaustive treatment, but perhaps enough to make clear that God is not unjust concerning those who died before Christ.

The Latin philosopher Cicero, who was not a Christian, once wrote,

If man enters a house or a gymnasium or a forum, and sees reason, method and discipline reigning there, he cannot suppose that these came about without a cause, but perceives that *there is someone there* who rules and is obeyed. How much more when he contemplates the motions and revolutions to be seen in the universe (*eg* the heavenly bodies) must he conclude that they are all governed by a conscious mind.

When St Peter went to the house of Cornelius, reported in Acts 10:34, he said,

I now see how true it is that God has no favourites, but that in every nation the man who is godfearing and does what is right is acceptable to him.

To come right up to date, Stalin's daughter, Svetlana, says of herself,

I was brought up in a family where there was never any talk of God. But when I had become a grown-up person I found it impossible to exist without God in one's heart. I had come to that myself, without anybody's help or preaching. But that was a great change to me, because since that moment my main dogmas of communism had lost their significance for me.

Surely St John was right on the mark when, speaking of the coming of Jesus in John 1:9, he described him as 'the true Light that *enlightens every man.*'

T. F. C. Bewes

Isn't it presumptuous to say that my sins are forgiven?

Yes, it is presumptuous to say that your sins are forgiven if you are no better than others but think you are. Indeed, it is worse than presumptuous; it is offensive to all decent people. But you do meet those who claim that their sins are forgiven and push religion down people's throats as if they and they alone know anything about God. Usually people like that once had a genuine religious experience and imagine that they are safe for ever, whatever they do. This brings down Christianity to the level of vaccination or knowing the password – and most intelligent people know that religion must be something more than that.

It is smug people like this who – as much as anybody else – get religion a bad name. Religion becomes the same as hypocrisy. The religious people themselves don't realize this, of course; they firmly believe that they are right, that they are in possession of God's truth. It is simply that they have never stopped to ask themselves what kind of people they really are. The men and women with whom they work could tell them in a flash, but they are probably too polite.

If religion has come to be just an empty belief, or if it is only a pale afterglow of something that was once too tremendous for words, then the best thing to do is to stop talking about it. It would certainly be wise to give up talking about your sins being forgiven.

When religious language is abused in this way it is of course a sure sign that some important truth is at stake. If religion means anything at all, then it must have something to say about the forgiveness of sins – unless God is a tolerant old boy who lets you off if you give him the right line of patter.

In the New Testament

When you look in the New Testament you find that Jesus forgave people their sins. (This was one of the things that led men to think he claimed to be divine.) In Matthew 9:1–8, for example is the story of Jesus saying to a paralysed man: 'Take heart, my son; your sins are forgiven.' Almost immediately afterwards he told him to take up his bed and go home. It is not surprising that the writer adds after this alarming event: 'When the crowds saw it, they were afraid, and they glorified God, who had given such authority to men.'

The man could scarcely doubt that his sins had been forgiven. Even without the astonishing fact that he could now use his legs, there was the fact that Jesus had spoken to him. He would never forget *his* words. You cannot escape the impression when you read the Gospels that when Jesus said a thing he meant it. If *he* said a man's sins were forgiven, then they *were*. That was the end of it. Jesus spoke with authority.

Certainty today

Nothing less than this kind of certainty is intended for men and women who live after the days of Christ. This is the implication of such language as: 'Therefore, since we are justified by faith, we have peace with God through our Lord Jesus Christ' (Romans 5:1), and: 'There is therefore now no condemnation for those who are in Christ Jesus' (Romans 8:1). Men and women who turn and believe the gospel need have no worry about their past sins. They are forgiven. God has said so. This is the whole point of the gospel as it is explained in Paul's letter to the Romans. Another of the writers of the New Testament even went so far as to say that he was writing to Christians so that they should be sure about this kind of thing (1 John 5:13).

But, you may say, Jesus has not spoken to me personally as he did to the paralysed man. How can I possibly have the same degree of certainty? Well, naturally we cannot meet Jesus face to face and actually hear his words of forgiveness to us, but in one respect we are even better placed. We can look back, as the paralysed man could not look back, to the crucifixion. We can see, as 1 Peter 2:24 makes plain, that in dying on the cross Jesus bore our sins and won our freedom. Ultimately the knowledge that we are forgiven rests on an event that took place in Jerusalem under the governorship of Pontius Pilate. We rest on a historical fact and on the significance given to that fact by the people who understood Jesus best. Our confidence rests on something outside ourselves.

Of course, you can be a Christian and not very sure about it. But the kind of Christian who is useful and who can help others to a faith in Christ is the kind of Christian who can humbly and fearfully say that he knows his sins are forgiven. There is nothing presumptuous in that – after all, what else can a man say when by the grace of God he has put his faith in Christ crucified, risen and ascended? He can scarcely say, 'I *hope* my sins are forgiven.' If you have been pulled out of a river half-alive and have been saved from drowning, you don't say, 'I hope I've been saved.' You say, 'I *know*.'

John King

23

Does God
ever lead people
into temptation?

Many people are puzzled by those words in the Lord's Prayer –
'... Lead us not into temptation' (Luke 11:4). Why did Jesus teach
us to pray like that? Does God ever lead us into temptation?

Temptation and testing

In answering this question, we must remember that in modern
English the word *tempt* suggests the idea of inciting a person to do evil;
but the root meaning of the word in the Old Testament is to prove,
examine, try, put character to the test. Thus the New English Bible
translation of the sentence in the Lord's Prayer is '... do not bring us
to the test.' Temptation, then, is anything, painful or pleasant, which
tests our loyalty to Christ and which, if we are disloyal, will lead us
into committing sins.

It is inconceivable of course that God, who is altogether holy and
righteous, and the enemy of all that is evil, should encourage us to sin.
How could he, who instructs us not to steal, suggest that dishonesty
could be justified at any time? Indeed James specifically states:

Let no one say when he is tempted, 'I am tempted by God,' for God cannot be
tempted with evil and he himself tempts no one; but each person is tempted when he
is lured and enticed by his own desire.   (James 1:13–14)

So God is never the author of temptation. Its author is Satan, who
uses every means (in alliance with the sinful nature within us) to relax
our loyalty to Christ, and to encourage us in disobedience and
self-indulgence. Satan is described as 'the tempter' (Matthew 4:3),
and there are many references in the New Testament to his subtlety
and powerful influence (see 1 Peter 5:8; Ephesians 6:10–12;
2 Corinthians 11:13–15, and others). In one of his parables Christ

speaks of him as 'a strong man, fully armed' (Luke 11:21). We deny his existence or underestimate his power at our peril.

Temptation and sin

Temptation itself, however, is not sin. It is quite possible to undergo repeated temptations without falling into sin. This in fact was the experience of Jesus Christ himself who was tempted in every respect as we are, yet without sinning (see Hebrews 4:15). Many who have newly become Christians are taken by surprise when, after their conversion, they find that temptation actually increases in intensity. And yet is it really so surprising, since in making Christ Lord and Saviour they are declaring war on Satan and his kingdom? It is the devil's chief business to trip the Christian up, to discourage him, to destroy his faith, and to render his witness ineffectual.

God is not the author of temptation. Temptation itself is not sin. It is yielding to temptation that is sin. And yet God allows the Christian to be tempted. Why is this? In order to prove and strengthen faith. The Bible is crowded with stories of people who were tempted – people like Joseph who suffered all kinds of trials and indignities, and yet who at the end could testify to his brothers:

As for you, who meant evil against me; but God meant it for good, to bring it about that many people should be kept alive, as they are today.　　(Genesis 50:20)

When a disappointment hits us between the eyes, or we experience some painful illness, or unpleasant persecution, what do we do? Blame God for it? This is our natural reaction. And yet we do wrong, for God has allowed it – not sent it – for our good. God greatly loves us and all his children and will never allow anything to happen to us which we are unable to bear. But he is anxious that we should mature into balanced and useful Christians, and one of the ways by which we grow is through the trials and temptations which come to us in life. So James can say:

My brothers, whenever you have to face trials of many kinds, count yourselves supremely happy, in the knowledge that such testing of your faith breeds fortitude, and if you give fortitude full play you will go on to complete a balanced character that will fall short in nothing.　　(James 1:2–4 NEB)

and again:

Happy the man who remains steadfast under trial, for having passed that test he will receive for his prize the gift of life promised to those who love God.

(James 1:12 NEB)

Meeting temptation

What matters, then, is not so much the nature of the temptations as what we do with them when they come. Naturally we shrink from such testings and trials. We would prefer an easy, untroubled path. But no soldier is fit for battle without hard training and some experience under fire. Expect temptation, therefore, but never yield to it. Combat temptation in the strength of Christ, never alone. Willingly accept trials as God's way of training you to be useful. Believe that victory is possible because Satan is a defeated enemy, through the cross. If you fall, get up and go on with Christ. Learn from your defeats, do not lie down under them (see 1 Corinthians 10:13; 1 John 1:9, 4:4; Romans 6:12–14; Philippians 3:12–14).

When you pray the Lord's Prayer in future, think of that sentence in this way: '*Lead us not to the place where we shall have to face trials and temptations, but if it is to be, deliver us from the evil one.*'

Richard Bowdler

24

Is the devil
a reality
or a myth?

A rather unconventional preacher once began his sermon in this unusual way: 'I am going to speak about the devil, and my subject has four divisions: *Who the devil is he? What the devil does he do? Why the devil does he do it? How the devil are we to deal with him?*' I dare say a good many of us have felt like that very often. We have heard it said that the devil is a myth, a personalizing of evil, a legend arising from the efforts of simple people to explain the mystery of temptation and wrongdoing. Yet somehow our own experience on the one hand, and the plain teaching of the Bible on the other, force us back again and again to the old-fashioned doctrine of a personality behind the evil – prompting it, cultivating it, suggesting it, compelling it – as alone satisfying the demands of our intellect as well as our instinct.

Who is he?
'The plain teaching of the Bible' – is it so plain? – introduces us to the devil as the serpent right at the beginning of Genesis (Genesis 3). We witness his final exit at the very end of Revelation (Revelation 20). And there can be hardly a page between without some reference to the devil and all his works.

He is described in all sorts of ways and by many titles. He is called 'the devil' (or slanderer); 'satan' (or adversary). In Revelation 12:9 we have a veritable thumbnail sketch of him in the words:

So the great dragon was thrown down, that serpent of old that led the whole world astray, whose name is Satan, or the Devil – thrown down to the earth, and his angels with him. (NEB)

He is also spoken of in Scripture as 'the father of lies,' 'a murderer from the beginning' (John 8:44), 'the Prince of this world' (John

12:31, 14:30, 16:11), 'the prince of the power of the air' (Ephesians 2:2), 'the evil one' (Matthew 13:19; 1 John 2:13), 'Beelzebub the prince of the demons' (Matthew 12:24). All this is far removed from a vague and impersonal influence of evil!

His origin is shrouded in mystery; but there are one or two quite intriguing glimpses scattered over the Bible, and from these it seems as if the devil was once an archangel (like Michael), and that he allowed pride to enter in, rebelled against God with a host of other angels, and with them was cast out of heaven. Now, with these demons, he is carrying on his wicked works until the final judgment. There is only one devil. When we read about *devils* the word is not the same in the Greek, and should be translated *demons*.

What does he do?

Although we know little, then, of his origin, we know a good deal more about his nature and character. The picture of the devil with horns, hooves, and a tail may well be a portrayal of his evil disposition; it certainly does not indicate the manner of his appearance to those he is seeking to overthrow. There are times when he is openly 'as a roaring lion seeking someone to devour' (1 Peter 5:8); usually he is transformed into 'an angel of light' (2 Corinthians 11:14).

'The devil is God's ape,' said an ancient writer; that is, he imitates God's work and tries to disguise wickedness so that it appears to be good and right. Jesus says he is a liar, a murderer, an enemy; he is described as a deceiver, an accuser, a tempter. One of the greatest proofs that the devil is not just a symbol of evil, or an evil influence springing up within us but is *some one* to be reckoned with, is to be found in the temptation of our Lord himself in the wilderness. There was no sin in him, so nothing from his own nature could have produced it; and such a deadly conflict as is recorded by both Matthew and Luke, and referred to by Mark, demands a real personality able to wrestle with the very Son of God.

Yet we must not ascribe to the devil the attributes of deity. He is not omnipotent – that is, he is not almighty as God is. He is not omniscient – that is, he doesn't know everything as God does. He is not omnipresent – that is, he cannot be everywhere at once as God is. He may have his demons everywhere, but that is another matter.

The devil's function is to mar God's creation and to destroy God's people. Peter tells us that he walks about seeking whom he may devour. The same devil who entered into Judas desired to sift Peter as wheat also, and filled the heart of Ananias to lie to the Holy Spirit. He snatches away the good seed from hearts in which it is sown, and sows tares amongst the wheat of God's kingdom. He hinders missionaries from doing their work (1 Thessalonians 2:18), sets out to deceive if possible the very elect as he deceived our first parents, and to ensnare the very leaders of the Church (1 Timothy 3:6).

How do you deal with him?

If you are a Christian, then you must expect the devil to make quite sure that his demons are constantly at your heels and dogging your steps. But never forget this: the devil is already a defeated foe. Even now, before his final overthrow, his activity is strictly controlled. Just as in the Book of Job he must still bow to God's permissive will, just as the demons in Mark 5 must gain Jesus' permission to enter into the swine, so the promise of 1 Corinthians 10:13 is positive and irreversible: 'God is faithful, and he will not let you be tempted beyond your strength.' We are told in Hebrews that Jesus became man in order

that through death he might destroy him who has the power of death, that is, the devil, and deliver all those who through fear of death were subject to ... bondage.
(Hebrews 2:14–15)

John in his first letter declares that it was for this purpose that the Son of God was manifested, that he might destroy the works of the devil (1 John 3:8). There is power in the Holy Spirit to give you victory, if you will but open your whole life to his control. You may know then what it means to be more than conquerors in him that loved us.

No doubt the devil would like to persuade you that he doesn't exist. Don't be deluded by such a gigantic lie. Put on the whole armour of God, that you may be able to stand against the wiles of the devil (Ephesians 6:13). 'Resist the devil and he will flee from you' (James 4:7). Jesus has conquered Satan not merely for himself but for us too. Recognize the devil for the enemy he really is, and then trust in the stronger than the strong to give you the victory again and again.

Desmond K. Dean

25

Has Christianity an answer to the problem of suffering?

Why does God allow undeserved suffering? To this intellectual problem Christianity gives only a partial answer. In the absence of a definite explanation by God we can only base our surmise on what we know of God's character. If, however, we are in the grip of personal suffering ourselves, we will not be very curious about this theoretical question. To us, suffering will not be a problem to solve but an experience to endure and to live with; and fortunately Christianity has an effective answer to this practical problem.

Is suffering the result of sin?
Doctors and nurses frequently hear people say, 'Why should this happen to me? I never did anyone any harm.' These people are convinced suffering is the result of sin, and yet they feel they have been as good as their neighbours. Of course, *some* suffering is the result of our own sin, but most physical suffering is not the direct result of it. This was clearly taught by Christ in a culture which attributed suffering to personal sin (John 9:1–3).

Suffering is part of man's environment in this world. God has put man into a world where he is at risk from injury as he learns by trial and error. If we fall from a height we are hurt; if we put a hand on something hot we are burned; any of us may be injured or killed by flood or famine, microbe or man. Far from saying, 'Why should I suffer?' a keen glance at the world around convinces a thoughtful person of the inevitability of suffering in this world, and the folly of expecting to escape it.

There is a third kind of suffering – that which is accepted voluntarily to help someone else, sacrificial suffering. Christ suffered for us on the cross in this way; he told his followers that they would suffer in the same way as they spread his message and carried on his work. This suffering for Christ, or for righteousness' sake, or simply in helping one's neighbour is 'by the will of God' (1 Peter 4:2–19). The Bible states repeatedly that it is God's plan for man to be in the battle and share the suffering. 'This will be your chance to witness for me' (Luke 21:13 *Phillips*).

Deserved suffering and suffering that a man chooses to undergo do not seem to worry most people, but now another question has to be faced.

Why does God allow the innocent to suffer?
In honesty we must recognize this problem and admit the great burden of undeserved suffering due to poverty, malnutrition, disasters, disease, and the selfishness of people. Nothing is gained by trying to belittle this paradox, that God who is loving and good has placed man in a world where the innocent often suffer.

The scientist faced with two apparently conflicting truths or facts has to hold them in tension until new light enables him to relate them satisfactorily. And this is what the Christian has to do with this problem. On one side of the coin is all the evidence of the Bible and from the life and teaching of Christ that God is good; on the other is the inescapable fact of innocent suffering. It is beyond our finite minds to understand why God permits tragic suffering which appears to have no possible beneficial result; yet we do know that Christ calls us to follow his own example in relieving useless suffering whenever we find it.

Can good come out of suffering?
Pain is one of man's best protections against injury. In fact it is such a useful danger signal that doctors sometimes delay relieving pain for a short while until they have used its characteristics to clinch the true diagnosis. In leprosy, which is characterized by loss of pain sensitivity, fingers and toes may be lost and blindness develop just because repeated minor injuries are painless and unnoticed. The ability to feel pain is essential to man's physical survival. Moreover, we do not need Christianity to teach us that suffering develops character. It can soften or harden a man, but virtues such as courage, patience, obedience, endurance, pity, and compassion cannot develop without it.

But the teaching of Christianity takes us further. The devil has a rather undefined place in man's suffering (working through natural means), as we see from Christ's temptations and from the stories of Job and the woman crippled for eighteen years (Luke 13:16); but his attack is only allowed up to a limit which is set by God's restraining hand (1 Corinthians 10:13).

Joseph came to appreciate that deportation by his brothers and years in prison, misrepresented and forgotten, were things God had planned 'for good' (Genesis 50:20). Paul states that his physical disability was to keep him humble (2 Corinthians 12:7). Peter pointed out to the early Christians that being harrassed by hardships was no accident; it was planned to test and develop their trust in God (1 Peter 1:6–7). The writer to the Hebrews emphasized that chastening, or child-training, was a constant feature of our heavenly Father's dealings with us (Hebrews 12:7–10); and we read that Christ himself learned obedience in the only possible way – by the things which he suffered (Hebrews 5:8).

Christianity does not teach us that God is so loving that nothing matters provided we are contented. Our passing happiness is not the end God has in view. Just as we would rather see our loved ones suffer in some measure instead of being content with contemptible and degrading circumstances, so God in love gives us what we need, not what we think is most desirable.

How should I meet suffering?
It is the set of the sails and the helm which determine whether a yacht sails securely into the teeth of a storm or is driven helplessly before it; so our attitude to suffering is more important than the force of the gale that batters us. How should we meet suffering?

Remember God loves you (Romans 8:38–39)
God who did not spare his own Son but gave him to die on the cross for you, loves you with an intense and eternal love. This is bedrock, the foundation truth for all who suffer. Nothing can separate you from the love of God, so rest in that love.

Follow the example of Christ (1 Peter 2:21)
Christ's attitude to suffering was seen supremely in Gethsemane and on the cross: it was one of humble self-surrender to his Father. 'Father, if thou art willing, remove this cup from me: nevertheless not my will, but thine, be done' (Luke 22:42).

Recall that suffering is a temptation and a challenge (James 1:2–4)
The devil uses it to wreck your faith in God and to make you doubt his

wisdom, love, and power. God uses the same experience to test and strengthen your trust in him. Paul, speaking of suffering, said that Christians were 'more than conquerors': that is, that Christ could bring us through it, not only undefeated, but richer for the experience of his love and power.

Douglas M. Jackson

26

If God is almighty,
why doesn't
he do better?

This is probably one of the biggest problems about religion that most people feel today. After all a 'mighty man' is someone who is successful, whether it is in war or business or sport, or any other sphere of life. He gets things done. He defeats his rivals on the way. Christians described God not just as mighty, but as *almighty* (all-mighty) and that means we should expect him to be successful, to be getting things done, to be defeating his rivals, not just once or twice but always, not just partly but completely.

But what do we see in the world? We see that most people are able to neglect or reject God and (apparently, at least) get away with it. And those who do support his cause don't always seem to be happy or to prosper. There is no *easy* answer to this problem, which has exercised some of the greatest minds of every age, but there are certain factors often forgotten which may help us to see it more in perspective. These factors refer to the past, the present, and the future.

God's work in the past

As far as the past is concerned, God has been successful but often in quite unexpected and unrecognized ways. He has created the world and sustained it, giving it those marvellous properties which the research scientists of the modern age are just beginning to discover. (Remember that science can tell us the 'how' of creation but not the ultimate 'why' and 'who.') More than that, he has dealt with man's biggest bogeys – sin with its guilt, and death with its fear. He has come among men in the person of Jesus, who was God brought into focus and plunged into the raging sea of human experience. Jesus has been through death, taking the consequences of *our* sin, and come out alive the other side of the grave, triumphant over all that evil could do. Millions have discovered that his death and resurrection can set them free from those terrible worries about sin and death (Hebrews 2:9, 14 *f*).

What about tomorrow?

There is a future too, according to the Bible. The time will come when the victory which he has already won will be turned into a complete and final triumph. During World War II, the day of the invasion of Europe by the allied liberating armies was known as D-Day. The success of their landings then and the superior strength of their forces made final victory over the Germans certain. But it was not until nearly a year later that fighting stopped and V-Day (Victory Day) was proclaimed. The D-Day of Good Friday and Easter is a certain signpost to the V-Day when 'death is swallowed up in victory' (1 Corinthians 15:54).

It is this sure expectation of ultimate victory which puts things in such a different perspective for Christians. It is much easier to endure hardship of every kind if there is a goal in sight (1 Corinthians 15:57 *f*).

God working today

This may not seem the real problem. Many people find themselves saying, 'Yes, but what of the present?' If Christianity refers only to the past, it is irrelevant history. If it refers only to the future, it is 'pie in the sky.' Well, we can see God doing plenty in the present if only we will look (Psalm 111:2). So much of what he does goes unrecognized. All modern discoveries are our attempts to understand his universe. Space-travel and all the rest are things which he has permitted us to learn. Through the research of scientists and application of their findings by surgeons and doctors, God is healing people every day. We are also learning how God makes it possible to heal the human mind through psychiatry, and many characters are being transformed through the power of the gospel. A host of people also who are suffering acutely can tell of God's goodness and his ability to supply all their real needs.

Suffering and freedom

'All right,' it may be objected, 'this sounds fine, but why is God not doing better? Why war, hatred, suffering and unbelief?' Well, suppose for a moment that all these things didn't happen. None of them has been produced by God, so it would mean that human nature and the world as we know it had changed. It would mean that there was no freedom for people if they always did right. They would merely be puppets in the hand of a God who controlled them mechanically. He would have won, not by love but by force. Once he allows human beings to be free, then he allows the possibility that they will spoil their lives and the world, that they will neglect or reject him. Would a married couple rather have children or puppets? The answer is obvious. For all the naughtiness and disobedience of the average child, he is far better than a puppet, for he can be loved and love in return. You can have relationship with him. So God wants to have a spontaneous loving relationship with us (2 Corinthians 5:14).

Our suffering too is bound up with the fact that we live in a fallen world. Yet the very fact of hardship and adversity is a fertile soil for the lovely flowers of courage, sympathy and self-denial. There is an old Arab proverb which says 'all sun makes a desert.' The life of the age to come will be all sun, but it will only be able to be appreciated by those who have drunk in this world the rains of suffering and disappointment (Revelation 21:1–4). It is possible to think of a world where these things never happened, but it would not be recognizable as the world we know with its temptations to evil and its challenges to good.

Can we do anything?
Why doesn't God do better? The answer is simply that he can't – that is, so long as he observes the limitations of the rules which he has set himself in the running of the world. But *we* can do better, and if we do we shall find the wonder of fitting ourselves in with his plan and discovering that it works. We shall find for ourselves that 'He has done all things well' (Mark 7:37). We shall look forward confidently to the time when he folds up the world as we now know it and introduces a world of perfection. Above all we shall find from our daily experience of his loving care that he provides all that we really need and that as we pray and live for him, his cause is seen to prosper in the world (Psalm 111:1–10).

R. E. Nixon

27

Isn't it irrational to believe in miracles?

No, it isn't. Why not? To answer this adequately there are two subsidiary questions we must first attend to. The first is: *What does the Bible mean by a 'miracle'?* (Naturally it is the *biblical* usage we must consider, not the popular one.) The second is: *Why do miracles constitute a difficulty?* When we have considered these we shall be able to see how, in the light of the Bible's revelation of the relationship between God and the world of nature, biblical miracles are not only reasonable but necessary. Let us take these two questions in order.

What does the Bible mean by a miracle?
In the Bible miracles are referred to mainly by three words which some translators have rendered *signs, wonders,* and *mighty works,* the three occurring together in Acts 2:22 RV and 2 Corinthians 12:12 RV, but being of frequent occurrence elsewhere. These three words enable us to see just what the Bible intends to convey.

A miracle is something which by its striking or unusual nature *compels attention* (it is a *wonder* – see for instance the story of Moses in Exodus 3:1–4, or John 12:9). However, the matter does not end there. If it did there would be little distinction between miracle and magic. Having attracted attention the happening *conveys a message* (it is a *sign,* as emphasized in John 2:11, 3:2 RV); and further, an important feature of the message is that *power is present,* and power of such a quality that it must be recognized as divine (it is a *mighty work* – our word *dynamic* comes from the same Greek root).

In view of all this, and of the biblical teaching that man is in bondage to sin (John 8:34) and on the road to destruction (Matthew 7:13), the role of miracle in the biblical revelation is rather like that of a neon sign reading EMERGENCY EXIT in a building subject to fire. It is designed to arrest attention, and to convey a message which if heeded will lead to life and liberty.

Why do miracles constitute a difficulty?
Undoubtedly in the main they do so because they seem to run counter to the picture of the world which science has given us. This is of a universe which exemplifies fixed laws, such as Newton's laws of motion, or Mendel's laws of heredity. These laws are our ways of expressing a quite fundamental conviction we have formed about Nature, a conviction often stated rather inadequately in the form: 'the same physical cause always produces the same physical effect'. When we release a stone it *always* falls; when we put a kettle on the gas it *always* grows hotter; when we bring together two suitable pieces of plutonium they *always* explode; and so on.

It is this regular behaviour of Nature that lies at the basis of our success in formulating scientific laws, and so of predicting physical events and harnessing physical forces. And the impressive achievements of science, both on the theoretical and on the practical level, argue in the strongest possible way that the scientist's conviction that Nature is *essentially* law-abiding is a valid one.

Now it is this conviction that a belief in miracles seems to undermine. Stones may usually be expected to fall, but on rather odd occasions they may quite unaccountably do otherwise! Or to take an example with more direct biblical reference, while the principle of the conservation of mass has proved its worth to countless investigators on numberless occasions, it constitutes a foundation much less satisfactory than supposed, for on more than one occasion it has failed, and failed spectacularly (2 Kings 4:1–6; Matthew 16:9–10).

On the face of it, therefore, belief in miracles does seem to put us in the intolerable position of having to question the validity of one of those fundamental principles on which not merely this or that particular scientific theory depends, but the very possibility of *having any science at all*. If Nature is *at rock-bottom* capricious and unpredictable (as miracles seem to suggest), the whole scientific enterprise with its reliance on law-abidingness becomes highly precarious. No wonder many scientists boggle at the miraculous!

The relationship between God and his universe
Before we pass on to see how the Bible provides for the validity of both science and the miraculous we must notice a common view, often held, of the relationship between God and his universe. This view

(spoken of as Deism) thinks of God as an expert clockmaker. Having made a superlative mechanism he now leaves it to tick on its own. If it goes wrong he 'intervenes' to put it right. It is such an act of intervention that constitutes a miracle.

Now while this view does make some sort of sense of both science and miracle (after all, clocks *do* operate according to very real built-in laws; and yet their escapement mechanism can 'slip a cog' and introduce an element of irregularity), it doesn't do anything like justice to the biblical revelation of God as Creator.

The Bible discloses that God is not just a clockmaker (who has given his creation more or less independent existence), but in some respects more like a great conductor of an orchestra on whose continuing activity the steady outpouring of the music depends. On this analogy the creation is like the sounding music. While the clockmaker can withdraw and the clock tick on, the moment the conductor withdraws the music ceases. This is what is meant by saying God is both *immanent* in his creation as well as *transcendent* over it (this view is called Theism); and the Bible very definitely teaches this (see very numerous passages including Corinthians 1:17 RSV; Psalm 104; Matthew 5:45, 6:26, 30, 32 – notice the present tenses).

The Bible's provision for the validity of both science and miracles

It is here that a very satisfying possibility exists of doing justice to the well-attested evidence for miracles without endangering the security of scientific foundations. It comes about like this. The Bible regards natural laws as arising not from the perfection of a mechanism (as the Deist does) but from the faithfulness of the Creator. Natural laws are our descriptions of what we observe of his mode of working, and because capriciousness is utterly foreign to God's nature (Malachi 3:6; James 1:17) the validity of Nature's laws is an ultimate one. To depend upon them is not to build in the least on a precarious foundation (see Genesis 8:21–22; Jeremiah 31:35–36). God knows that man's life would be impossible were he not able to rely on Nature; if, for instance, pressure on the pedals of his cycle caused movement in a quite unpredictable direction. Accordingly, in his faithfulness he maintains constant the pattern of his workings in the realm of mechanics, and Newton's laws of motion appear.

But this insistence on the faithfulness of God to man's needs has other implications. What if man is, since his fall (as the Bible asserts), an abnormal creature 'alienated from the life of God,' 'lost' and 'perishing' – should not the very faithfulness which guarantees science mean that God will take extraordinary steps to meet man's extraordinary need? Of course it does, and it is very significant that biblical miracles are all associated more or less closely with man's redemption from the slavery of sin, from alienation, to renewed fellowship with his Maker. It is in this light especially that we can view such great miracles of redemption as the Exodus, the Virgin Birth of Jesus Christ, and the Resurrection.

Thus we reach the conclusion that the validity of the scientific enterprise is enhanced rather than weakened by the Bible's teaching on miracles; both the regular order built upon by science, and the 'supernatural' which is the anchor of faith, are expressions, in response to different needs of man, of the very same attributes of God: his faithfulness and love.

Douglas C. Spanner

28

Can't you be a Christian without going to church?

He was a small boy in a deserted playground. On the wall there was a chalked wicket, and with a tennis ball he was steadily bowling at the wicket. Did he *need* to play in a cricket team, to be a cricketer? In one sense, no, because he was still a cricketer, even when he was at solitary practice, although after ten minutes he tired, and wandered off. In another sense, yes, just because the essence of cricket is that it is a team game, or a corporate activity.

Can you not be a Christian without going to church? In one sense you can, because going to church doesn't make you a Christian, and staying away doesn't automatically deprive you of your status as a Christian. There are five reasons, however, among others, which should encourage us, or help us to encourage others, to be regular at our church attendance.

The family reason

'There is no such thing as a solitary Christian,' said John Wesley – meaning that our faith in Christ is not only to be worked out in witness to the world, but lived out in love and friendship together with our fellow-Christians. It is an odd family that arranges for each member to have Sunday dinner alone, in a different room in the family home.

The early Christians discovered that an intensely personal trust in Christ ('Repent, and be baptized every one of you in the name of Jesus Christ' – Acts 2:38) led to the corporate life of the Christian family demonstrated in regular 'church-going' ('And day by day, attending the temple together...' – Acts 2:46). The Bible's emphasis on personal faith leading to Christian family worship is built into the early annals of Christianity; see, for example, Ephesians 3:14–15, 5:19–20, and the description of Pentecost itself in Acts 2.

The teaching reason

Christianity is a school as well as a family, and the ordained ministry of the church teaches the faith of Christ to its members. This can best be done when the congregation is together in church on Sunday, even though specialist groups will obviously receive intensive training at other times elsewhere. The early apostles appointed 'deacons' (*cf* Acts 6:3) over practical church administration, so that they could give themselves 'continually to prayer, and to the ministry of the word' (Acts 6:4). God obviously intended that his people should be instructed for 'his gifts were that some should be ... pastors and teachers, for the equipment of the saints, ... for building up the body of Christ' (Ephesians 4:11–12).

The Church is not only a family meeting in its home, but a band of scholars gathering in its school, and we are 'truants' if we are absent.

The training reason

The Christian receives truth, so that he may share this treasure with others: 'Thou therefore endure hardness as a good soldier of Jesus Christ' (2 Timothy 2:3 AV). Christ's soldiers need not only personal guidance, but tactical and strategic training, so that:

> Like a mighty army
> Moves the Church of God.

We meet in church to intercede for God's warriors in the great battlefields of the missionary world, to learn how to overcome Satan, our enemy, by the weapons of Bible-study, prayer, and attendance at the Lord's supper and to take military council together for the battle for good in our own parish.

The scholar must not be a truant, the child must not be a prodigal son, and the Christian soldier should avoid being named as a deserter:

No soldier on service gets entangled in civilian pursuits, since his aim is to satisfy the one who enlists him.   (2 Timothy 2:4)

The balanced reason

God has planned a rhythm of life, which makes us balanced, well-oriented people. Night and day, winter and summer, rest and work, all emphasize this. One day's rest in seven is 'a perpetual obligation and divine decree,' said Bishop Daniel Wilson. God's day is for rest, so that we may be refreshed and in it quietly worship God, our Creator, Redeemer and Sanctifier. Out of love and gratitude to him, and especially in commemorative thanksgiving to Christ our Saviour, who rose on the first day of the week, we should be in God's house and at his table on Sundays.

In addition, the pressures of modern living demand the rest of Sunday quietness; and the concentration on material necessities during the six days of the week calls for a preoccupation with eternal truths in God's house on Sunday.

The biblical reason

Lastly, the Scriptures call for our attendance at church, just because we are Christians: 'Not neglecting to meet together . . . but encouraging one another' (Hebrews 10:25). Christ set us an example in his own synagogue attendance: 'He came to Nazareth, where he had been brought up; and he went up to the synagogue, as his custom was, on the sabbath day' (Luke 4:16). He tells us that we must worship God in spirit and in truth: 'for such the Father seeks to worship him' (John 4:23). He sets us an example, and bids us worship God who desires our worship.

These five reasons listed above are strong indeed, but our reaction to them often helps us see our own spiritual condition more clearly. A young Oxford undergraduate, who after a long period of agnosticism had finally committed his life to Christ, and found him as his Saviour and Lord, said to me at the start of his confirmation preparation, 'Churchgoing, from being a weak *ought to*, has become a strong *want to*.'

Could your reaction to the question at the head of this chapter be symptomatic of the reality – or superficiality – of your relationship to Jesus Christ?

Maurice A. P. Wood

29

Does God
want our worship?

Worship is the outgoing love of a human being expressed in words, thoughts, or song to the God whom he has learned to know and whose friendship has become a reality to him. Many people think there is no benefit in public worship, and we may well ask whether there is a real value in such a spiritual activity in a world crying for material benefits.

The purpose of worship
First of all, our worship brings gladness to the heart of God – not because he wants us to praise him in the way human beings like to be flattered, but because he really is *worthy* of praise and that he knows that when human beings offer him their gratitude and love, they are most truly being themselves and bringing benefit to their own souls by experiencing inner unity with him who is ultimate truth. Worship is a cleansing agent of the human spirit. It brings us back to ultimate realities and from being an intensely personal spiritual exercise, it overflows to others, so that the worship of people together is greater than the sum of the individuals.

True worship, however, is not confined to the singing of hymns or psalms in church. It is bound up with the life of the world outside, and as we put before God the needs of that world and the problems facing it, we are driven to become ourselves the answer to our own prayers and to go out in service of others. Thus worship becomes practical. Prayer and praise bring a sense of awe, and the committed Christian finds himself driven by the Holy Spirit with a deep desire to worship both alone and with those who, like him, are wanting to live for Christ.

How should we worship?

Human beings are so different and their temperaments so varied that there must be many different ways allowed for Christian worship without any one group claiming the totality of 'rightness.' Generally speaking, though, worship can only come from facing ourselves in repentance, facing God in faith and trust, thanking him for his great benefits, meditating on his character, and from this finding our hearts full of praise and joy. Worship of course includes prayer for people, for causes, and for things that we need, and finally the acceptance of power and an experience of unity with the Father, the Son and the Holy Spirit.

Worship thus unifies us with ourselves and stops that disintegrating conflict which is within us all. It brings us into a relationship of love with our fellows, even those who are not worshipping with us. It gives us a kinship with the world of nature, and, above all, a sense of the presence of our Lord.

Difficulties of worship

Few could claim that those principles that have been expressed above are a daily experience in their lives. Our own materialistic concerns and wandering thoughts, the busy interruptions of life itself, the lukewarmness of our own devotion and of many church services, are a constant drag on our prayer life. The lack of enthusiasm of other Christians, for which each of us bears part responsibility, tends too to drag us away from 'the good that we would,' and so we neglect it, to our cost.

To overcome these difficulties each Christian must make his own rule of life, which will take different forms, but the inner 'creative pause' or 'quiet time' each day is an essential part of the Christian life, for Bible reading, prayer, and perhaps above all, deep meditation. The experience of real fellowship with other Christians often results in a renewed and spontaneous desire for worship. Christian work, when we are seeking to serve our fellow men, is also a great help in driving us to our knees and to the fellowship of other Christians, which we all need so much.

Above all, if we depend more and more on the Holy Spirit we shall find that he urges us to worship, both alone and with others, and perhaps especially in the service of Holy Communion when we meet in a living way the Christ who comes to dwell within us. The Lord's own service on the Lord's own day should surely be central to every worshipping group of people, whatever their denomination or church tradition.

Recent developments in worship
In recent years there has been a reviving movement of the Holy Spirit which is bringing new release in worship and breaking out of the old boundaries of liturgical and formal services. This at times produces extravagances of utterance and praise which can be 'off putting' to the outsider and disturbing to the members of a congregation, and the movement needs careful leadership and self control. Yet the new spirit of jubilation and thanksgiving can and often does bring a fresh reality and converting power into hitherto staid and unimaginative services.

The urgent need is to channel this joyous spirit away from extravagances and the shibboleths of some kinds of evangelical piety and irrelevant or thoughtless 'Hallelujah' expletives into inspiring worship and strong and popular music which may appeal to the heart without shallowness of doctrine or of intellectual content. There have been some splendid 'breaks through' in the publications of *Youth Praise, Psalm Praise, 100 Hymns for Today* and Sydney Carter's songs, to name a few.

O. K. de Berry

30

Is Holy Communion really so important?

Just how important is Holy Communion? After all, there are bodies like the Quakers and the Salvation Army who seem to manage without. Is there perhaps a danger that it can be over-emphasized? Of course, *anything* can be over-emphasized if we lose our sense of proportion. Holy Communion is not the *only* means of grace: there are Bible reading, prayer, fellowship, and other ways of drawing on Christ's strength. All the same, the Communion *is* very important.

The Lord's own service
How can we neglect it when Christ himself commanded us to observe it? At the Passover Feast, the most important festival, which no Jew would ever think of missing, Jesus took the bread and wine that were on the table, gave thanks, broke the bread, and said, 'This is my body which is given for you. Do this in remembrance of me.' And as he gave the cup he said, 'This is my blood of the new covenant. Do this, as often as you drink it, in remembrance of me.' Surely at such a solemn moment, on the very night before his betrayal, he meant his words to be taken seriously?

Just as the Passover was the great feast of the People of God under the Old Covenant, celebrating their freedom from the bondage of Egypt, so the Lord's Supper was to be the great feast of God's people, his Church, under the New Covenant, celebrating their redemption by the blood of Christ.

The Church's practice
It might be argued that the Passover was celebrated only once a year. Does this not suggest that Holy Communion ought to be a great

annual celebration? All we can say is that the first Christians did not understand it that way. The picture we have of their church life is that 'they devoted themselves to the apostles' teaching and fellowship, to the breaking of bread and the prayers' (Acts 2:42). Paul had to rebuke the Corinthians for certain abuses at the Lord's table, but he never suggested that they came together too often. And we can say with certainty that they met for the breaking of bread at least every Sunday. The Lord's own people came to the Lord's own service on the Lord's own day.

In our time the Church is returning to this ideal. But two words of caution are needed. First, in emphasizing the sacrament we must not squeeze the ministry of the Word into insignificant proportions. A proper use of the new forms of service will help to ensure that preaching the Word of God is not neglected. Secondly, the frequency of Communion must not cause us to neglect the preparation of ourselves beforehand by self-examination, repentance, and renewed faith.

All things new
When Christ rose from the dead the New Age began. He made new men, a new community – his Church, a new literature – the New Testament, a new day – for the new community changed the old Sabbath to the day of resurrection, and a new service – the Lord's Supper. Every Sunday is to be for the Lord's people a day of renewal at the Lord's table.

Renewed faith. Our salvation depends upon what Christ has done for us in his atoning death and glorious resurrection. But we easily forget. Our hearts grow cold. In the Lord's Supper we have 'a perpetual memory of that his precious death.' As Paul said, 'For as often as you eat this bread and drink this cup, you proclaim the Lord's death until he comes' (1 Corinthians 11:26). As we take part in the breaking of bread, our faith grasps afresh all that our Saviour has accomplished for us.

Renewed strength. We do not only break bread in remembrance of Christ; we take and eat, we drink the wine. Jesus said on that first occasion, 'This is my body. This is my blood.' We know that we are eating and drinking bread and wine, but faith in Christ's word makes us aware that he is feeding us spiritually with his own body and blood, his very life. We remember his words in John 6:48, 'I am the bread of life.' So we feed on him in our hearts, and our strength is renewed. What a feast! It is the Lord's Supper indeed.

Renewed love. Of course our love for God is renewed as we partake of all that *his* love provides. But more: our love for one another is strengthened. The Lord's Supper can never be a merely private act of devotion. It is Holy Communion, which means exactly the same as holy fellowship. As we partake of the one loaf and drink of the one cup we demonstrate to ourselves and to each other that we are the Body of Christ. Like members of the human body, we belong to each other. We are one, not because we happen to like each other, but because we all belong, sinners though we are, to the one Saviour. Because he has accepted us, we accept one another, and are willing to *be* accepted by all the others in this Holy Communion.

Renewed consecration. God accepts us as we are, but not to leave us as we are. Our joint participation in all that Christ has done for us must lead us to yield ourselves afresh to him in gratitude. One ancient name for the Lord's Supper is the *eucharist*, which is Greek for thanksgiving. As Christ has sacrificed himself for us, so we offer and present ourselves as a living sacrifice to him. Every communion service should be marked by a happy consecration of our lives.

Renewed hope. 'You proclaim the Lord's death *until he comes*.' We celebrate Christ's victory on Calvary, knowing that one day that victory will be complete. 'We look for his coming in glory.' It must often seem to us that the cause of Christ is losing ground, but every time we come to the Lord's table our hope is renewed. We affirm afresh that Christ will triumph in the end, and because we are his we are on the winning side.

Is it really so important? The Lord commanded it. His Church has faithfully obeyed all down the centuries. In doing so millions have found renewal of their faith, their strength, their love, their consecration, their hope. If we neglect Holy Communion are we trying to be wiser than the Church? Or than the Lord himself?

Martin Parsons

31

Why are my prayers
so often
unanswered?

That's a fallacy for a start! I don't deny it may often *seem* to be like that, but your prayers *are* answered, you know.

Look at it this way. If your idea of prayer is simply telling God what you want – a shopping list with 'Amen' at the end – then for a start you've got prayer wrong. Prayer is not, and never was, meant to be a magical way of seeing that you get the job you're after, or the boy you think you're head over heels in love with, or the money to pay the rent man, or anything like that.

It's not so much getting what *you* want as asking God to give you what *he* wants. Even Jesus prayed 'Your will be done' when he spoke to his Father. In his letter, James, the brother of Jesus Christ, says:

You don't get what you want because you don't ask God for it. And when you do ask he doesn't give it to you, for you ask in quite the wrong spirit – you only want to satisfy your own desires.　　　　　　　　　　　　　　(James 4:2,3 *Phillips*)

Two reasons for failure

Here then are two blunt reasons why our prayers don't seem to produce the goods. First, because we don't really ask in faith. That means that we don't believe God *can* answer this particular prayer even though we say it, just in case! Secondly, all too often, as we've already seen, we only ask for things to please ourselves, whether they are good for us or not. God answers the first kind by ignoring it because frankly it isn't a real prayer at all. And he answers the second by saying 'No'. So, because men always tend to blame God when things go wrong, we say, 'He hasn't answered my prayer' when he certainly has! It's just that he hasn't answered it *our* way.

But for lots of Christian people who genuinely want to please God as best they can there is a deeper problem. Suppose you say, 'I've prayed for my friend to become a Christian but nothing seems to have happened.' The object sounds good enough. You want a person to come into that real experience of the forgiveness and love of God. Surely that kind of prayer ought to get a 'Yes' from God? As Paul writes:

... this is undoubtedly the right thing to pray for; for his purpose is that all men should be saved and come to realize the truth.   (1 Timothy 2:3, 4 *Phillips*)

But hold on a minute. No doubt the prayer is a proper and Christian one but you've left one thing out. Either man has a free will to disobey the purposes of God or he is a puppet. But both the Bible and human experience tell us that man is a great deal more than a puppet. He can frustrate the will of God. He very often does. So the effect of prayer is all bound up with the purpose of God and man's rebellious attitude towards him. It may be that your friend will respond to God's love in twenty years' time – an answered prayer nevertheless. It may be that as far as you can ever know he does not respond. Yet God still answered your prayer for *he* was faithful because he did not deny your friend the right to be a human being with a free, if twisted will. It probably grieves him far more than it grieves you to see a man reject him. But that is the terrible responsibility which man chooses to lay upon himself. Through all the choices of life – great and small – he *can* choose a fearful destiny for himself if he is foolish enough to want to do so.

The point of prayer
What then is the point of praying? Surely the only answer to that must be that God tells us to because he wants us to learn to depend on him and to align our needs and wishes with his will.

Remember, prayer – real prayer – doesn't come marked down at sale-prices. It is in fact, a desperately expensive business – expensive in time, in giving, in loving. Maybe we don't seem to experience much comeback from God because we don't ever 'give' as we pray.

And don't forget this. Even if God does sometimes answer our prayers with a 'No' or a 'Wait' there are countless other times when the answer comes through loud and clear – 'Yes!'

John's first letter sums it up very well. He writes:

We have such confidence in him that we are certain that he hears every request that is made in accord with his own plan. And since we know that he invariably gives his attention to our prayers, whatever they are about, we can be quite sure that our prayers will be answered.   (1 John 5:14, 15 *Phillips*)

That's the attitude to take if you are puzzled about what seems to be unanswered prayer. That's the attitude called *faith*.

Michael Saward

32

As I have been baptized, do I still need to be converted?

The short answer is probably 'Yes,' because if you don't know whether you need to be converted or not, the odds are that you do.

But there is more to it than that, and much confusion of thought, and one of the reasons why, maybe, is that the word CONVERSION is used to describe a considerable variety of differing spiritual experiences. Take Peter, for example, in Luke's account of the Last Supper. '... when thou art converted,' said Jesus, 'strengthen thy brethren' (Luke 22:32). But was he not already, at least to some extent, a converted man? Had he not responded long since to the call of Christ and left everything to follow him (Mark 10:28)? In what sense, therefore, had he still to be 'converted'?

Again, what of John Wesley's experience, when on May 24th 1738, at a meeting in Aldersgate Street, London, he felt his heart 'strangely warmed'? A professing Christian from his earliest days, a man of prayer and godly discipline, an ordained minister of the Church – such indeed he was, but on May 24th 'a seeker became a finder,' says J. E. Rattenbury. 'A devout Pharisee became an Evangelical Christian. A man who had the form of godliness received its power. A zealous servant of God, to use his own words, became a son.'[1]

It can do no harm therefore to notice that the word 'conversion' occurs only once in the whole of the Bible: in relation to 'the conversion of the Gentiles' (Acts 15:3). And when the verb *to convert* is used, it means simply, according to Dr. Erik Routley, 'stopping, turning, attending, and pursuing a new course.' Sometimes it is used in the active and sometimes in the passive sense, implying both the idea of deliberate choice and commitment, and also the idea of submission to the will and power of God.

But conversion has also to do with a new beginning, a new birth (John 3:3–8), a new life (2 Corinthians 5:17). And here baptism, especially the practice of infant baptism, adds to our confusion, for baptism has also to do with a new beginning, a new birth, and a new life. In fact there are two rival views on this question of the beginning of the Christian life, according to Bishop Stephen Neill, and this is what he says about them:

Conversion is the beginning of real Christian life. Christian nurture, education and worship may be valuable preparations. But no one is, or should be, called a Christian until he has personally encountered God in Jesus Christ, until he has personally repented, until he has personally accepted God's gift of salvation through Christ... The reality of the Church in every generation consists of those who have thus been born again.

That is one view. But Christian life also

begins at baptism, when by the grace of God operating through the Church original sin is taken away, and the divine life is sown as seed in the heart of man. Through Christian teaching, through life in the Church, and through the grace of the sacraments, this seed can grow. Though growth may be hindered by resistance on the part of the individual, nevertheless it is a continual process. To demand any other decisive new beginning is to deny the reality of the grace of God. What the individual is called to do is to recognize the reality of what God has already done in him and take that seriously.[2]

There is the other view.

Happily, we do not have to choose between these two points of view. Each is rooted in New Testament teaching, and in the Church of England we are committed both to the reality of baptism *and* the necessity of conversion. But there is a distinction between the two, for many a man who has been baptized stands in need of conversion, and many a converted man, who has already become 'a new creature,' has still to be baptized.

Perhaps the best way of distinguishing between baptism and conversion is to see them in terms of emphasis. In baptism, the emphasis must ever be laid upon what *God* does. In conversion, the emphasis rests upon what *man* does: upon his 'stopping, turning, attending, pursuing a new course': upon his being turned about. So baptism, 'is the public denial that salvation can be won by man's own efforts – it is not of works, lest any man should boast. Manifestly it is the gift of God,' says Bishop Joost de Blank.

'Baptism is a sacrament and its fundamental character is sacramental. That is to say it is something which God does, and not something that we do'[3] – a truth most marvellously illustrated by Jesus' teaching about the new birth (especially in John 3:5: 'Unless one is born of water and the Spirit, he cannot enter the kingdom of

God'); for what baby was ever born of his own volition or was ever aware as he entered the world of what was happening to him?

'If any verse in the Bible is sacramental,' writes Douglas Webster, 'this is the one. It is an exposition of the meaning of Christian baptism as the mode of entry into the new life. As physical birth is unconscious and we are not aware of its happening, it is not unreasonable to suppose that spiritual regeneration may be unconscious also – a very different thing from conversion, which is a conscious turning to God.[4]

Nevertheless, there must still be conversion: the deliberate disposition of heart and mind towards God and away from the things that are not of God, a voluntary act of committal and surrender to Christ and his claims, a willing response to his call to follow and the *turning* of the natural man into the spiritual man, the man of this world into the man of God. Yet both baptism and conversion mark only the *beginning* of the Christian life; the beginning of a process that will not be complete 'until Christ be formed in you' (Galatians 4:19).

Geoffrey Lester

1 *The Conversion of the Wesleys* by J. E. Rattenbury (Epworth Press, 1938), p. 35.
2 *Scottish Journal of Theology* (December 1950), p. 359.
3 *This is Conversion* by Joost de Blank (Hodder & Stoughton, 1937), p. 33.
4 *What is Evangelism?* by Douglas Webster (Highway Press, 1959), p. 166.

33

What is meant
by the
social gospel?

Not many years ago Evangelicals commonly used this term in a distinctly disparaging sense. This was not primarily because those whom they regarded as preaching and practising the 'social gospel' put such a strong emphasis on the social *implications* of the 'good news,' but because they seemed to regard the social causes which they championed so ardently as themselves constituting the *essence* of the gospel – as, in fact, the term itself implies. And this was, and still is, a convincing reason for objecting to the term and rejecting the attitude of mind which it epitomizes.

The Christian and the world
But it must be recognized that a further reason why Evangelicals used to shun the whole concept was because of the prevalence of a form of pietism which led many of them to compartmentalize their lives, and to feel that Christianity as such should be almost exclusively concerned with the cultivation of their own spiritual well-being and the attempt to win individuals for Christ out of a corrupt society – and then to foster their spiritual growth in the same pietistic tradition. They were to be separate from the 'world' not only in the sense of resisting the seductions of a society and way of life which left God and his commandments out of account, but also in the sense of any personal involvement in the struggle for social and economic justice, moral standards, and the duty to participate with their fellow citizens in their political obligations. They also emphasized the fact that their own true citizenship was in heaven that they failed to realize the implications of the fact that they had at least a 'lodger's vote' here on earth – and that the same Book which exhorted them to snatch

individuals 'as it were from the fire' also commanded them to be the 'salt' and 'light' of the society out of which these individuals were to be snatched. But we must always remember that one reason for this attitude was that they had been largely forced on to the defensive; and a beleaguered garrison finds it desperately difficult not to have a somewhat restricted outlook.

Times have now changed in some ways but not in others. Most Evangelicals have moved away from an excessively pietistic attitude, and there is now, happily, a widespread recognition that it is unbiblical – and positively sinful – for a Christian to attempt to contract out of anything that the command to love his neighbour as himself properly implies, or to fail to fulfil any of his civic obligations.

But there is also, unhappily, a new concept of 'salvation' (as in the current slogan 'Salvation Today') which uses the term 'reconciliation' *primarily* of the removal of barriers between man and man rather than the reconciliation of sinful men to a holy God, and which interprets the New Testament message of 'liberation' primarily in terms of deliverance from political, social, economic and racial bondage rather than the guilt and power of sin.

Theology of revolution
In its most extreme manifestation this takes the form of what has been called the 'theology of revolution.' Sometimes, with S. G. F. Brandon, it depicts Jesus himself as a Zealot, or with Harvey Cox, sees God as pre-eminently present in the life of the 'secular city' and its political events and upheavals, or with Richard Shaull, Father Cardommal and many others, proclaims the duty of Christians to be involved in the social revolution as it develops, since it 'is only at the centre that we can perceive what God is doing,' and can make a 'revolutionary rupture with a society based on injustice.' Those who think in these terms believe passionately that the basic duty of the Church is to 'bring in the kingdom,' and that this primarily involves, as D. R. Sharpe puts it, 'an undying determination to get the will of God realized in the organized life of every man and woman' and to bring 'every aspect of corporate as well as individual life ... into accord with the law of divine justice, mercy and love.'

This sounds splendid. But how can the corporate lives of individuals who have known a personal conversion and radical regeneration be brought into captivity to the divine will? This represents a contradiction in terms which results, presumably, from a failure to recognize the fact that social injustice ultimately springs from the basic sinfulness of individual men and women who are alienated from God – just as the 'theology of revolution' continually ignores the fact that it is not *only* the rich and the oppressors, but also the poor and the oppressed, who fundamentally suffer from the same malady.

Creator and Redeemer

What, then, does the Bible teach on this subject? It teaches, as I understand it, that God is both our Creator and our Redeemer, and that it is the duty of the Christian to witness to him in both capacities. As Creator he made this world and loves the men and women he created in his own image. He still cares that hungry people should be fed, and homeless people housed; that the moral decay of society should be held in check; that suffering should be alleviated, conditions improved and crime, cruelty and war restrained. In other words, God still has a message for society as such – a message which was passionately proclaimed by the Old Testament prophets, exemplified in the life and teaching of Jesus, and reinforced by his apostles. So it is the Christian's task to witness to this, by his life of practical involvement and by his testimony to the commands and purposes of God.

But man has not only oppressed his fellow-men; he has also become alienated from the life and fellowship of God himself. So God the Creator became God the Redeemer, and in Christ he came to seek and to save the lost – not *primarily* through his life of perfect obedience to the will and purpose of God, but by his death of vicarious atonement for both our personal and our social sins. And it is the duty and privilege of the Christian to witness to this by seeking to bring the message of God's unfathomable love for the sinner to the whole world for which Christ died. It is not a question of 'either/or,' but of 'both/and'; for we cannot contract out of our duty to society by our care for the personal salvation of individuals, nor out of our duty to evangelize by our concentration on the much wider meaning rightly attributed today to the word 'mission.' There is, indeed, a very real sense in which mission to man in his temporal needs, however essential in itself, is bound to be inadequate without the primary message of what God has done for his most basic need of all – forgiveness and regeneration – through the cross of Jesus Christ; for it is this latter and nothing else which secures for man his eternal well-being, and it is only through a radical change of individual hearts that the health of society can most effectively be promoted. Not only so, but as Alec Vidler has pertinently written:

This hoping, this looking forward, this waiting and watching – not for a new order on earth, a new social 'set-up' in history, but for the consummation of the kingdom of God at the end of history is fundamental to the Christian outlook. One of the deplorable features of modern Christianity ... is its loss of conviction as to the primacy and ultimacy of the eternal order of being, and therefore its natural but pathetic wish to have its hopes and ideals realized in this world. This is just what the Christian man, of all men, ought to know can never be the case. There can be only partial, fragmentary, transitory realizations of the kingdom of God in history. We must certainly work for them with all our might, but it is not upon them that our hope depends.[1]

Norman Anderson

1 *Christ's Strange Work* (SCM, 1963), p. 65.

34

Is there an essential difference between a clergyman & a layman?

The simple answer to this is 'no.' There is no essential difference between them: that is, there is no difference *in essence*. But there are other differences, which we should know and understand. They are differences of function and role.

Ministry in the Church
The Christian Church consists of those who are united to Christ by faith and are called to serve him. That service we call 'ministry.' It belongs to the whole Church, and not just to one part of it. The invitation, to every member of the apostolic church, was 'Come to Him ... and like living stones be yourselves built into a spiritual house, to be a holy priesthood, to offer spiritual sacrifices acceptable to God through Jesus Christ.' The writer then goes on to describe the People of God in these words: 'You are a chosen race, a royal priesthood, a holy nation, God's own people, that you may declare the wonderful deeds of him who called you out of darkness into his marvellous light' (1 Peter 2:4, 5, 9).

In the light of this the word 'church' does not equal 'ordained ministry.' The Lambeth Conference of 1958 expressed it, 'Ministry and laity are one. There may be a difference in function but there is no difference in essence ... There could be a revolution in the life of the church if this truth could be rediscovered.' Let us remember that if the whole is priestly, then the individual parts are so as well.

Diversity of Ministry
The New Testament picture is of diversity within unity. 1 Corinthians 12 makes it plain:

There are varieties of gifts, but the same Spirit; and there are varieties of service, but the same Lord ... To each is given the manifestation of the Spirit for the common good ... For just as the body is one and has many members, and all the members of the body, though many, are one body, so it is with Christ ... Now you are the body of Christ and individually members of it.   (1 Corinthians 12:4–27)

Every part of the body is equally important and necessary. Indeed, if we were to speak in terms of 'higher' and 'lower' positions, God would remind us that 'the parts of the body which seem to be weaker are indispensable,' and that 'God has so adjusted the body, giving the greater honour to the inferior part' (1 Corinthians 12:22, 24). Equality, however, does not preclude subordination, and this we find in the church. Of course, we find it first of all in the Godhead. Christ is co-equal with the Father, but is subordinate to him. The pattern of equality with subordination is a basic concept in the Bible.

The clergyman's role and function is different from the layman's. This can be seen from Scripture passages such as the following:

Take heed to yourselves and to all the flock, in which the Holy Spirit has made you guardians, to feed the church of the Lord which he obtained with his own blood.
(Acts 20:28)

We beseech you, brethren, to respect those who labour among you and are over you in the Lord and admonish you, and to esteem them very highly in love because of their work.   (1 Thessalonians 5:12, 13)

If a man does not know how to manage his own household, how can he care for God's church?   (1 Timothy 3:5)

Remember your leaders, those who spoke to you the word of God... Obey your leaders and submit to them; for they are keeping watch over your souls, as men who will have to give account.   (Hebrews 13:7, 17)

The Ordained Ministry

These passages mean that ordained ministry in the church is not to be regarded as something like a club secretaryship. It is God himself who calls a man to ordained ministry: the church ratifies that call, and gives it public authorization. Ordained and lay ministers, together, form the Church of the living God.

It is sometimes called an 'equipping' ministry (following Ephesians 4:12). There, its purpose is described as 'for the equipment of the saints, for the work of ministry, for building up the body of Christ' – *ie* it is to teach and train the people of God for their life, and work and witness.

Another aspect of the work of the clergy is that they are authorized to act publicly in the name of, and on behalf of, the whole church. The laity are not. God is a God of order: the picture of anyone and everyone taking upon himself to do whatever he thinks the church should do, is not attractive, and is far from what we find in the New

Testament. If a man is to act on behalf of the church as a whole, it is reasonable, and scriptural, that he should do so only on the authority of the church.

Again, the clergy are set apart for the study of God's Word, and for prayer. Of course, these are a normal part of the life of all Christians, but the clergy are particularly charged with these because of their function as teachers of God's people. In the nature of the case, their job gives them greater opportunity for these things.

The whole subject might be summed up in the succinct comment of one writer, who says, 'The laity are not helpers of the clergy so that the clergy can do their job, but the clergy are the helpers of the whole people of God, so that the laity can be the Church.' We are united in a common Master, in a common service, for a common purpose – the glory of God, and the salvation of all men.

J. C. F. O'Byrne

35

What ought we to do about people like Jehovah's Witnesses?

Well-established religious sects like Jehovah's Witnesses, Mormons, and Christian Science have been active in this country for many years. There can be few homes that have not been visited by Jehovah's Witnesses or Mormons, and few people who have not come across Christian Science with its strange views regarding sin and sickness.

More recently such sects have been joined by newer groups such as the Children of God, Guru Maharaj Ji and his Divine Light Mission, Armstrong's 'Plain Truth' movement, and Scientology. These sects are all anxious to spread their beliefs and can be both persuasive and plausible as we meet them on the door step, at the street corner, at public meetings or exhibitions, or through their literature. What ought we to do about them?

Understanding their beliefs

First, we should try to understand what they believe. Some of them (eg Jehovah's Witnesses and the Children of God) claim to be *Bible-only* groups, maintaining that everything they believe, their codes of behaviour, and even their methods of organization and outreach, are based entirely upon the Bible. Others (eg Mormons and Christian Scientists) are *Bible-plus* groups, maintaining either that they possess further divine revelation contained in extra scriptures (like *The Book of Mormon*), or that they have received further spiritual insight through which to interpret the Bible (eg Mary Baker Eddy's book *Science and Health*). Some claim another personal incarnation of God, who is to us today what Jesus was to people 2,000 years ago (eg Guru Maharaj Ji). Yet others claim to fulfil the aim of all religions and philosophies and to apply their wisdom by means of scientific techniques (*eg* Scientology).

Space does not allow us to look at any of these sects in detail, for each group has its own elaborate doctrinal system. We must simply note that in practice most of them reject major Christian doctrines regarding God, Christ, and salvation, and some of them hold strange views concerning the second coming of Christ and the end of the world.

Jehovah's Witnesses say that God is one person (Jehovah), that Christ is a secondary god who once existed as the archangel Michael, that the Holy Spirit is God's impersonal force at work in the world, that Christ's death freed us only from the sin of Adam, and that Jesus' second coming took place invisibly in 1914.

Mormons believe that God has a tangible body of flesh and bones and once existed as a man, that the difference between Jesus and ourselves is simply one of degree, for we are all potentially gods, that living Mormons should be baptized on behalf of their dead relatives to help them gain salvation, and that there are at least three grades of salvation (or exaltation, as they call it).

Christian Scientists believe that God is impersonal (Truth, Spirit), that the Christ is the divine truth which has always existed but which is seen at its best in the man Jesus, that sin and sickness are unreal, illusions, mirages, and that deliverance from both comes about as we recognize their unreality and concentrate our thoughts on God.

The Children of God believe that separation from the world means that they must forsake their parents and their employment to live together under rigorous discipline in communes which they call colonies. They are expected to give absolute allegiance to their seniors within the movement.

Guru Maharaj Ji teaches his followers in the Divine Light Mission that he is the contemporary avatar or incarnation of God (thought of as Cosmic Energy), that salvation comes through 'taking knowledge' of God, and that only the Guru or one of his lieutenants (known as Mahatmas) can impart this 'knowledge.'

Scientology, which describes itself as an applied religious philosophy, believes that all human problems are caused by 'engrams' (mental pictures associated with traumatic experiences) and that liberation comes when, through an expensive course of question and answer sessions, the afflicted person is encouraged to bring these engrams to the surface. The movement also holds many strange views which have more in common with science fiction than with mainstream Christianity.

Most of these sects are totally opposed to orthodox Christian churches and some (especially Jehovah's Witnesses) regard Christian clergy and ministers as the paid servants of Satan. Although they differ widely from each other in their beliefs, almost all the sects agree that the orthodox Christian Church no longer represents God, for soon after its founding it became apostate. After that, no true Christianity existed on the earth until it was restored through their founder – Charles Russell in the case of Jehovah's Witnesses, Joseph Smith in the case of Mormons, Mary Baker Eddy in the case of Christian Scientists, and so on. Though they claim to accept the teaching of the Bible, they often distort its meaning either by taking verses out of their context or by re-translating them in ways that support their own doctrinal standpoint. Another common characteristic is their rejection of the Christian view that salvation is God's free gift, received through trusting Christ and not obtained by good works. Some of them think that they are earning salvation as they knock on people's doors, sell their movement's literature, or proselytize in other ways.

Learning from them

Secondly, we should respect them and be willing to learn from them. In my experience, spanning twenty years of study of the sects and contacts with sect members, they are at least as sincere in their religious beliefs and practices as most Christians. They sincerely believe that they have found God's truth by becoming members of their sect. It is also worth remembering that many of them have turned to sects after failing to find what they were looking for in the Christian churches. Often the sect has attracted them by its close fellowship, the strong sense of security it gives its members, and by the clarity with which it expresses its beliefs. Within the membership of their sect, individuals have been made to feel that they are important.

Church members need to take a hard look at their own church fellowships in the light of these important factors. We can all learn from the sects, and not least in respect of the zeal with which they seek to spread their teachings. An ordinary Jehovah's Witness spends at least ten hours a month witnessing from door to door. Mormon youngsters are ready to give two years of their life at their own expense to serve as missionaries. As Christians we can respect their sincerity, even though we believe they are sincerely wrong. We should also covet their zeal.

Helping them

Thirdly, we should love them and pray for them. It is easy for us to regard sect members as enemies and to treat them accordingly. We ought to treat them as we would treat other non-Christians. They are our brothers and sisters for whom Christ died.

Fourthly, we should be ready at all times to offer them what we have in Christ. If they keep strictly to the beliefs of their movements, most sect members do not have (and many of them do not profess to have) a personal experience of Christ as Saviour and Lord. They do not believe that by the grace of God they have been born again. They know nothing of the inner peace that comes from opening one's heart to Christ. As Christians speak to members of sects, they should remember this and be ready when the time is ripe to testify for Christ. Do not allow yourself to become involved in a heated argument about side-issues like blood transfusion and drinking coffee. In particular, do not join in what can best be described as 'Bible ping-pong,' an exercise in which texts, usually torn out of context, are bandied about between you. There may be occasions when you may usefully discuss details of belief and practice calmly but frankly, if you have taken the trouble to discover what the sect to which your contact belongs does believe, but by far the most effective approach, in my experience, is to tell him what you know of Christ and what he has done for you.

Maurice Burrell

36

Why is religion so dull?

It all depends what you mean by *religion*. And then, of course, it all depends what you mean by *dull*.

If by religion you mean worship, ritual, public prayer, and all the paraphernalia of organized systems of belief, then *dull* is probably the wrong word. A Hindu procession may be supersitious, old-fashioned, and reactionary, but it is hardly *dull*. Nor is Salisbury Cathedral, or St Paul's, or St Peter's, Rome. True, religious music is regarded by many as dull, but others (often irreligious people) consider it exciting and stimulating.

Is Christianity dull?

Christianity *can* be dull: that is to say, organized Christianity can. There *is* a drab, grey dullness about much formal English religion, for instance: the cold buildings, the lifeless singing, the droning parsonical voice, the listless, bored 'worshippers,' the apparent irrelevance of it all to real life in the real world. This – we are not disposed to labour the point – could be considered dull.

Why? How has this happened? Why should so much English church-going be a dead, dull, meaningless thing, as cold and unexciting as a wet Sunday (and notice the simile)?

Was it always like this?

After all, no one could describe the Christianity of the New Testament as dull. You don't have to believe in him to agree that Jesus Christ is one of the most *interesting* people who ever lived. There is nothing dull or grey or tepid about *him*, whether quelling a riot or healing a cripple or raising a corpse or calming a storm – or preaching a sermon. They didn't nod off when Jesus of Nazareth was the preacher.

The early Church, too, could hardly be described as dull. Read the Acts of the Apostles! Here was a community throbbing with life, thrilling, energetic, dynamic: it was feared, hated even – but never ignored. They had their problems, of course. But they were the problems of life. Today, our problems are all too often the problems of death.

What has gone wrong?
The infant Church had 'favour with all the people' (Acts 2:47 RSV). People dared not join the Church because of the tremendous spiritual power it displayed, but they held the Christians in high honour (Acts 5:13). The Church's 'image' was of a revolutionary, dynamic body, led by men who were described by their opponents as having 'turned the world upside down' (Acts 17:6).

There are places today where the Church is regarded in that way, but not very often in Britain. The New Testament picture contrasts very vividly with the academic, nominal, 'respectable' religion which is practised by so many of us today.

But generally where Christians – in Britain or anywhere else – really take God at his word, really put their trust in Jesus Christ, and really try to be led by the Holy Spirit, something like the picture in Acts is reproduced. There is nothing dull about biblical Christianity. The Holy Spirit is the 'Life-giver.' Jesus Christ came to give to those who received him *life* – and life in its fullness (John 10:10). When the Church takes the Bible seriously, obeys God, and is led by the Spirit, its problems will be over-enthusiasm, exuberance, indiscipline (as in the Church at Corinth in New Testament times) – not boredom, monotony and drabness.

What is the answer?
Individually it is, surely, to reject mere 'religion' and accept the gospel, to ignore the trappings and go for the heart of the matter, to turn from outward forms and traditions and enter into a relationship with God through Jesus Christ that is the most vivid and real thing in all the world. When we have found Christ we shall be able to put the outward forms and symbols in their right and proper and helpful place. But to have them *without* the inward reality is to have all the dullness and frustration of a menu without a meal. After all, a wedding service can be boring, but marriage should never be – it is the relationship that really counts.

In the Church, the answer must be a return to the faith and life of the apostolic Church. Dullness comes when the edge of Christian challenge is blunted, when 'keeping the wheels turning' is the main ambition, and not shocking or upsetting anybody is the chief aim. But joyfully to seek the Holy Spirit, gladly to accept the commands of Christ, and enthusiastically to proclaim the good news of a Saviour from sin: this may be (for some) extreme, 'emotional,' profoundly disturbing – but it can never be called *dull*.

David Winter